Corpexit

Free yourself from the Corporate Grind

By

Y Not

For E and our children,

you are the sunshine in my life.

CONTENTS

'Life is either a daring adventure or nothing. To keep our faces towards change and behave like free spirits in the presence of fate is strength undefeatable.'

Helen Keller

A NOTE FROM THE AUTHOR

Naively, I thought that leaving the corporate world would herald the immediate start of a bright new dawn and that all avenues forward would become clearly visible once the main blocker of 'corporate servitude' was removed. I assumed that lots of meaningful activities would fill my time, however, the obvious next steps did not manifest themselves so easily. Instead, I came to the uncomfortable conclusion that there was work to be done here to sift out the real existential guidance coming from my own gut versus the robotic set of expectations and constraints that I had become so conditioned and used to living with. These unconscious constraints not only limited my options but also my view on life to such a degree that the voice in my head was more often than not the voice of the corporate, rather than my own.

I have written this book to enable me to work through my very own worker-loo which started the day I made the decision to leave corporate life. I had little awareness of the flood of emotion and basic life challenges that would follow what I viewed as a life-liberating decision. I have a desire to share my experience with others who may be considering their very own corp*exit*. I want to let them know that they are not alone and that for me the process of letting go had many highs, and indeed lows, as I found myself navigating choppy, uncharted waters where I often felt I did not even have the vocabulary or means to adequately deal with the inward turmoil and external impacts this type of life-levelling change brings with it.

In doing so, I offer a toolkit of sorts, along with a workbook which has become part of my daily routine, helping to constantly steer me out of my own internal quagmires and unconscious patterns, nudging me forward each day. I hope it helps you find comfort and to pro-actively take the steps which can help you sift through your social conditioning so you can listen to your own internal voice which knows exactly what you need, and why.

I take the opportunity to look at how the corporate world works and how current corporate culture adversely impacts us workers.

I finally give myself leave to imagine what a utopic working world might look like – *dare to dream!*

During my journey, two characters surfaced with whom I 'play' in this book as a way of exhibiting how we are often torn within ourselves, especially when confronted with real life impacting choices. These are:

- my soul / creative director: gently persistent, supportive and my guide on the path to creativity

- my ego / agent: loud, opinionated, rule-based and the gatekeeper of my basic survival needs

You can choose to read the book sequentially or just dip into selected chapters that resonate on any given day. I have summarised all of the chapter reflections and tasks in a single workbook at the back of the book for your convenience, should you want to use it in that way.

Good luck with your journey and know that on your quest, the universe supports you!

CHAPTER 1

My Corporate Journey

Working in a corporate is something I have done since leaving college at 20 with my shiny university degree; but little did I know that I would be running for the hills 30 years later, asking myself why the hell I had signed up for corporate life in the first place?

In the nineties, having a degree was seen as a rite of passage, and to win a corporate job was a natural next step to bettering yourself and increasing your social circle. Thrilled to become a member of a professional organisation, a body of people all working towards a common overarching purpose, I spent the next three decades moving from one company to another, seeking that next ever-better career move, more money, more status, bigger teams, more power. My ego was stroked each time I won an interview and I happily moved up the corporate ladder from dogsbody to team leader, then manager to global head in my final role. By the time I reached this last senior-ranking role in a global multinational, I was deeply entrenched in corporate culture to a point where I found it often overrode my own internal narrative. This was compounded by continual social training (or ritual brainwashing as I see it now) to ensure full compliance with the corporate ethos, which is essential to successfully navigating corporate life and which I accepted enthusiastically.

In particular, as a senior manager I understood that I was expected to tow the company line and ensure my teams did so also; those that didn't where routinely weeded out through the performance review process. Ascending to higher roles gives you the illusion that you are driving your own career forward and you are on the corporate pig's back, for you are the one that guides, that plans, that wields the power of change (or so you think), and the power to hire and fire. As a leader in your field, you thrive on the feeling that your voice matters (the reality is that your boss's voice and in turn *their* boss's voice matter even more) and, regardless of how in control you feel, the corporate strings are being pulled all the time by someone more powerful, often working toward a much more elusive corporate agenda.

An important directive for the corporate manager is entrainment of the team to achieve the goals laid down by the very senior members of the organisation, without question and at whatever cost. Working in the corporate world for the last three decades in many different types of organisations, I realised that fundamentally they all harbour the same set of rules and expectations. Each may use different language and different tools for enforcing the corporate policies and behaviours, but ultimately everything you do is guided toward corporate compliance and protecting the shareholders – you are a cog in the wheel providing whatever it takes to ensure that a glowing profit margin is sustained and if that means selling your soul, then you can most certainly sign up for that in exchange for a healthy corporate wage and title.

Full entrainment of your ideals with the corporate ideology is a necessary step if you want to move up to the pinnacles of seniority in the organisation; there is little room for independent journeying here even though you may feel quite ardently that this is not the case, that the company embraces innovative thinking, change and individuality but ultimately every outcome is driven by that share price. It was when I reached the peak of my career that I realized that I had encountered what I can only think of as a type of glass ceiling; I had always thought of this as a mythical construct but in fact it appeared very real. A mental impasse required me to stop and consider if I really wanted to ascend further by joining the ranks of the über-senior team, a small curated group who are tasked with working to the agenda handed down by the corporate board and ultimately had no room for my individualised approach. Thus, feeling I could no longer use the experience I had gained over the decades in any creative or meaningful way, unbeknownst to myself I began kicking off the slippery dissolution of my corporate buy-in. Like someone on the brink of leaving a cult with a head full of conditioning, an array of fresh new thoughts and questions began to plague me night and day, questioning me on what exactly I had bought into and why I was choosing this path. *Could there be another?*

My corporate timeline

My corporate career-span entails a broad mix of corporate sectors from manufacturing to healthcare to insurance and banking. I have always felt that it is healthy to pivot in life, to keep growing your skills and broadening your horizons. Starting out in my corporate career, I was thrilled to join the ranks of the adult workforce. After a lifetime in education as a penniless student, to finally start to earn my own way felt like I had arrived. I was completely open and ready to invest my life energy into eking out a successful corporate career as well as developing a corporate family of friends (many of whom I am still friends with to this day). I never asked myself why I should choose a corporate career: coming from a modest, working-class family a job in corporate-land seemed like winning the golden ticket to a better life, one where the wolf would be kept from the door and one where my growing ego could be validated. It was at this point that I made an unconscious agreement to serve the corporate entity, relinquishing my human hours of creativity in exchange for the hallowed corporate pay cheque.

To me, the journey from one role to the next reflected my personal growth and acquisition of new skills within the technical arena, the expansion of which seemed essential to climbing the corporate ladder. All of this seemed to me a perfectly natural thing to want to do and as long as it was making me happy, then I would continue to follow the trail unquestioningly. As life started to get more complicated in my mid-30s with the arrival of a partner, children and a mortgage, those *Why?* questions finally started to pop up. I would routinely bat them away, due in part to the little amount of time I had to do any real navel-gazing and also due to the necessity to make ends meet, especially when I became the household breadwinner after my partner had a major medical episode. You do not tend to question things when you are in 'fight or flight' mode and so the years passed until eventually pockets of time started to open up along with periods of burnout. All the while, my growing disenchantment with the song-sheet I had signed myself up to quite willingly in lieu of a corporate title, corporate pay cheque and corporate security had weaved itself into my family life and my unconscious thinking to a level that I was not aware of until I finally stopped to take a look at the drivers for my unhappiness and lack of overall well-being.

It was only when I had reached my late 40s that I decided it was high-time that I started to identify and prioritise what I wanted to do about the rut I had found myself in and how I would go about changing things without toppling the whole deck of cards that was so precariously stacked on my family's monetary need. I had, over time, architected a way of living that at its core was fundamentally not sustainable or sufficient to meet my true life needs either for me or those of my partner or my children.

With what I can only think of as moments of awakening or consciousness, you start to realize that it is to your own detriment to rationalise everything through the lens of money. What's more, I feel we are actively groomed to foster this distortion of money's hold on us in our modern society. We are often seen and evaluated as the sum of our material belongings, and colleagues will share with glowing deference about so-and-so who is earning an eye-watering six figure salary as if they are the hallowed one among us. I cannot help but feel that we are worth so much more than a monetary sum and that we owe it to ourselves to step outside and smell the roses, or at least figure out how to cultivate some before it's all too late and we end up dis-eased, dis-contented and dis-oriented with whom we are.

So, another decade closes and here I arrive at the brink of a new one, feeling excited about what the new opportunities and learning that this mortal unhooking from the corporate space will afford me and those I care for. I am excited to reveal the chapters that are still to be written in my own life story.

Reflection

My career journey thus far has centred on corporate life. In a way, I have been shaped by this experience over the last 30 years but I truly believe we amount to more — we tend to think we are comprised of just a mind and body that function to meet the need of our basic material existence. I believe we also lay claim to a soul, the often deep, inner quietened voice that holds the key to our own true wisdom. Stepping out of one well worn chapter to start another fills me with both anticipation and a certain amount of trepidation. Considering how 'what you do' colours and shapes your life, I feel I am well overdue a change of tyres to start a new adventure into the unknown whilst carrying with me the learning from my previous experiences. Just taking that first step was all I really needed to commit to before I finally started to feel the return of a flow and ease, which oxygenated my being whilst signalling me forward in search of new shores.

Task

Draw up your own career journey to date — what does it tell you about your journey so far? What pivots may be necessary for your growth and ease? When looks like a good time to take your first step?

CHAPTER 2

A Slow Release

Once I started asking those 'why' questions of my work choice, ugly truths about the societal value of my corporate toil started to surface and, in reaction, my disengagement from work ensued. An undeniable sense of unease and dissatisfaction with everything in my life deepened in the pit of my stomach each day. I noticed my dreams becoming drained of colour so that soon I was more often than not dreaming in only black and white, if at all. I had minor palpitations as work deadlines loomed, and issues that surfaced as part of the daily grind seemed to affect me more deeply with passing time, to a point sometimes that I felt completely exhausted and debilitated by it all. This unease would literally start on a Saturday evening when I started to ready my being for a return to the ship on Monday morning. The sense of unease continued and worsened as I got to Sunday night, to a point where I would literally feel like vomiting. So, either I was just not coping or maybe I didn't like what I was starting to see once I took the time to really look? I started to work with a career coach with whom I hoped I could disentangle the threads of my unhappiness from what once felt like a fully invested and glittering career. Time with the coach only served to clarify the cause of my discontent, for it did not sit with my work as I feared but with me not finding the working panacea I desired within my own organisation; rather, I unveiled as I peered deeper all of the mental constraints imposed by my choice of work. Challenging these constraints seemed to only aggravate my work situation further. The career coach gave me an opportunity to see things from a broader perspective, objectively positioning the idea that maybe this was just how the organisation needed to function and it was me that needed to change my approach. So, I had a choice: either I could choose to run with the wolves or change tack entirely. It's funny when you already know what you want to do, deep down, that gut instinct never fails to nail it but yet it takes someone outside of ourselves to reflect those same feelings and thoughts back to us to be able to see the wood for the trees.

I had been writing in a journal on and off for over a year now, mainly about the steps needed to leave my job, endlessly weighing up the pros and cons of leaving corporate life. There's no doubt I found this exercise to be both terrifying (*How would I ever survive without the safety net of the organisation behind me?*) and thrilling (*What if I could really make it work on the outside?*)

Weary from every work week, eventually all of the pent-up frustrations started to smoulder like a ticking time bomb; it was there inside me, waiting for something to set it all off. Unwittingly, the situation came to a head when I fell ill. In a very unexpected way, illness gave me the space to step back from the circus that had become my daily grind and initially switch off while my lungs fought for oxygen just to keep breathing and my body entered a new state of weariness; coma-like, I was literally stopped in my tracks, suspended whilst all of my bodily resources fought off the hostile entrant. Slowly, as my immune army started to win little battles, parts of my being started to come back online – first my mind which had just been in fight or flight mode, started to whir again. The ego's rasp unmistakable in the battlefields, still waging: *'You need to get yourself ready to go back to work! Who do you think is paying for all of this? Did you think you would just lie here forever?'* As the drip feed of daily nagging continued, I realized that apart from being physically so sick, I just couldn't even contemplate getting up to go to work. There was a growing wardrobe of terror of work-related things yet to be done that had to be dealt with and worked through. Facing it all head on, I eventually acknowledged that I simply did not have the strength to take that mantle of woe back on. Not just that, but also a new feeling stirred within, a new voice, gentle but firm and surprisingly uncompromising: *'I don't **want** to take all that back on again; it does not serve me well.'*

Well, that made me stop and think, so lying there, I started to ponder what that would mean for my career, my family and my mortgage, and very quickly I spiralled into a state of high anxiety as I allowed all my worries to congest the truth that my system had surfaced. The ego threw the book at me but still I could not let go of this chink that presented itself to me. I decided to do something I had not done in such a long time; with my energy low, it just involved sitting up straight in bed. I cleared my mind as best I could, and set myself up to meditate on this new conundrum that overtook every other thought in my throbbing head. Slowly but steadily, I started to feel a sense of calm as I breathed in and out, trying to eradicate all negative thoughts and worries from my mind-space, letting them slip away and then posing the question: 'What should I do?'

Two words came back quite clearly in response:

'LET GO.'

The simplicity and humility behind these words resonated heavily. I just knew then that I was guilty of holding on to it all too tightly, for binding up expectations and outcomes to every permutation, coupled with my endless lists of things to do; so much so that I could hardly breathe or sleep without tying myself up into further knots. Letting go of all of it would not end my life, would not be so disastrous that I could never recover from it, and yet for all those months I lay there, struggling with it.

Letting go seemed like the only reasonable way forward if I was to serve me and my soul's existence better, more fruitfully. There surely had to be more to living than this? I began to reflect on my pre-career aspirations and interests, when I was unmarred by the clawing needs of the ego, the attainment of material things, the upward career climb to reach an ever-higher status; to meet the approving looks of my parents, friends and work colleagues; to give my children 'the life I never had' (nor never knew I needed!). I had got completely caught up in the hamster wheel of what being successful looked like in modern society, without once giving any thought to whether I was successful in terms of being truly happy. That younger me was free and courageous and aligned with herself but I had allowed myself to be driven by an ego that I should have tempered – where had the balance gone? No wonder I ended up a writhing mess: I was completely at dis-ease with myself. How could I keep going on this path when I understood that it would eventually manifest as a very real disease in my physical being? So there it was – the most basic driver of all: self-preservation, the underlying driver to allowing myself to LET GO.

This was to be the unchallengeable rationale I would use to counter the ego, a simple way of me explaining to the world that I simply couldn't continue on this course as it was. It would continue to make me sick so I called time on this chapter. It simply was time for me to let go and change tack.

Reflection

Identifying your unconscious patterns and expectations of yourself and allowing yourself to let go of those that no longer serve you is critical to our personal development.

Task

What are you undertaking in your work life that makes you feel unhappy? What do you think you could you do to alleviate it? What would happen if you simply let go? Write out the impacts and benefits to clarify for yourself.

CHAPTER 3

Closing the Door

So here I am: unemployed and alone; well, not quite if you count the partner, the dog, the cat and the teens downstairs.

Creating this space was the hardest thing to do in my head, always finding something else to divert my attention and to stop me from having to get here, 'here' being the start of a clean slate, because now that I *am* here, I don't really know what comes next both in terms of this output and my life … psychosomatic, I guess.

Weeks back, as illness struck, I had no idea that I would not be returning to work. When it came to the day where I should have been returning to the fold, I wondered to myself for a mere moment really: what if I didn't go back? What then? I had been harbouring this fantasy for nigh on two years with innumerable permutations of how we might make things work financially if I did leave the inner torment that had become my work life, because in all honesty, work day on work day it was getting harder. Beneath my smooth corporate-suited exterior, my soul literally felt like it was in the grip of some ravenous, dream-eating monster which wanted to bury itself in the core of my being, having torn strips of flesh and flayed its way to the remaining warmth, my beating heart ... so this sickness was the mask that my freedom wore, I just didn't know it at the time. This fleeting thought opened just for a bare moment a vista of ease and well-being, a slice of dream-life where harmonious good eclipsed all the low self-esteem and self-doubt that had increasingly begun to plague me as I climbed ever higher on the ragged corporate rungs. So, there I lay, day-dreaming while I sweated things out and I finally allowed myself the thought, 'Why not?' and just like that, after months of agonising navel-gazing, I acquiesced, responding to myself, 'Why ever not?'

The thoughts of returning to an ever-demanding group of work stakeholders, the needs of a growing team, the regulatory needs of a burgeoning global business, all seemed to conflict with that very peace that somewhere in my core, my very essence was clinging onto. *Why Not?* What was the worst that could happen? That I might get well, that I might let these ever-growing terrors just drip away, that I might be able to look at my own family without counting the seconds that I had free to speak with them? All that guilt suddenly mounted its own defence in this battle between the corporate will and my will / my need, and my need was stronger, more urgent, and it demanded from me an answer right there on the precipice of turning fifty. So, there it was, my inner soul laying siege to my alter-ego which feared letting go of the corporate reins, title, invested time, and money, and in contrast my ego was no match for the want of the soul – all this under a sweating and exhausted mantle of worn-out flesh. So, I made the break, simply telling my boss I wasn't coming back in order to focus on getting well which was true on so many levels.

I was giving myself permission to let go.

Of course, this process did not happen easily; I lay claim to a lot of baggage around my work life which had to be dealt with, not least with the context of turning fifty and what that meant. Leaving a comfortable, senior ranking, high paid job – to pursue *what?* I had no plan, no immediate idea of a way forward, just a notion that there in the very moment of my life I couldn't keep doing what I had been doing for the last thirty years anymore, the rationale being there just had to be something better out there for me and how would I ever find out what that might be if I didn't stop what consumed me night and day so that I could look into the jaws of life and really find out what might improve things for me and, ultimately, my family who had to live with me.

So, this book is about that journey – how I managed to let go, a process I am sharing in case it helps you too.

Reflection

Closing the door on the corporate life is akin to leaving a cult: you need to hold on to all of the things you could do once you close that door.

Task

What do you imagine the blockers to leaving the corporate space might be for you? How would you feel? What mindset will help you to override those feelings to enable you to move forward?

CHAPTER 4

An Emotional Roller-Coaster

The Fear

Day one of the rest of my life, was not the day of days that I thought it might be, lying in bed eating the grapes of freedom I had gifted myself by pressing *send* on a resignation email, to my now former manager. No, it was fraught with pure unadulterated fear, of the kind that viciously chews on your guts while setting your heart racing faster than it ought. A sweeping fear with waves of anxiety which almost paralysed me as I endeavoured to throw myself forward into the monstrous churning chasm of the unknown that could eagerly sweep me away. I couldn't think straight or reason with it; no, my alter-ego, that she-devil minx, was in full-flow to show me the error of my ways. *'You thought you could simply let go of all that, of your work, and that would just be it?'* chided the ego maniacally as I, on my knees, tried to comprehend the enormity, the repercussions, of what I had just done the day before …

Naturally, the reflex when you do something that feels cataclysmically in direct conflict to your immediate well-being, is to simply undo it, go back and say it was all a delusion, go back and say you're sorry, you didn't want to rock the boat like that (at this, the ego smiles with beguiling relief as she pushes you ever more toward the precipice of your decision), but somewhere inside you, a quiet voice whispers, *'No! What you did was right and justified and not just essential for your very well-being but your future life on this planet depends on that door staying shut now that you have so firmly slammed it.'*

But the ego won't let up with you there! Oh no, she is just getting started as she sharpens her claws with her reason and intellect; she will make you sorry you ever entertained the thought, she will run at you with the full force of all the logical reasons why you should be on the other side of that door, not here alone in this empty hallway with no idea which door you are supposed to open next. The next few weeks continued in this oscillation of whether to go back or move forward. Reason suggested through my own mind voice (the ego) *that living without an income with two teenagers at school was just utter madness and that I must tout de suite get back on the workhorse immediately before the mould of disuse sets in. If you won't go back to your old job, then pick up the phone and get yourself a new one ... yes, go and polish that resumé, your LinkedIn profile, your interview outfit – you can't simply just stay here in this hallway and do nothing! Who do you think you are? Why are you different to the other 99% of the working population? What gives you the right to think you can just walk away from all of this? You're not yourself, you're not at all well, you should ring the doctor, ring work, ring the agencies ... Get yourself back in the ring, girl ... it's only the 10th round, you have come through much worse, you're a fighter this is what you do ...*

Then the seduction: *Oh think about the salary, the holidays, that holiday home, that car, bigger, better things that you can have if you stay! What will you have if you leave? Nothing, that's what, absolutely nothing and, worse still, you will be no one, a nobody out there, walking the streets. Your kids won't talk to you. Do you think for one minute your friends will want to know you? People will laugh! And think about your poor parents! What will they say or think? You're the one with a high-ranking job — how are they going to cope if they get wind of this? What will the neighbours say? You will be a laughing stock. You can't just simply give up and think no one will have anything to say about it — you have responsibilities, you have people who depend on you, people who look up to you, people who need you. You can't, you can't, you can't … You simply cannot do this to yourself, to all of us … it's suicide.*

And so it went on for weeks and weeks: the ego ranted and raved like a wailing harridan, wanting nothing more than for you to undo it all and just stay as you were … completely stuck.

Reflection

Our ego is embedded to keep us 'safe' whilst being stroked so we become addicted to it. It will navigate toward the easiest route each and every time.

Task

What does your ego cling to, to keep your world 'safe' and harmonious? What feels unsafe to you and why? What might happen if you override your ego?

Grief

The depth of this feeling rattled me; the grieving actually felt as if someone close to me had died. Here I was, mourning the loss of my former self, my team (they had been a truly wonderful team), my network, my standing in the world, my meaning for living. It was a *lot*, I can tell you; there seemed to be no end to the depths of which I sank lower and lower each day. I'm sure the sickness didn't help but the exhaustion seemed to merge into a heavy weight that just trapped me squarely under the guilt and shame of severing all connection with the world I had lived in from 7am to 6pm every day for decades.

The corporate world felt incredibly real to me: it represented all of my worries, my highs, my responsibilities. In fact, my corporate day *was* my life – I freely admit this – with my family life tacked on around it. Oh, I worked very hard to blur the lines around the tacking, to make myself believe that I had a 'work-life balance', to make myself believe that in fact my home life was *more* important to me than work, however, my dreams, my racing heart when the phone rang or my email notifications beeped told me otherwise. I was completely beholden to the corporate, and like a nodding dog I needed to continue smiling and saying the right things to those on the outside of my corporate bubble, to make myself believe that yes, you could have it *all* and nothing or no one would feel short-changed.

Increasingly, however, I realised before D-Day ('departure day') that everyone including me was being short-changed in my life and that brings with it a good deal of pain, especially when you see it in the faces of your own children who know, yes, they *know* that Mummy is too busy to deal with your xyz today because she has a really important job so you don't matter until Friday afternoon at 3pm when you will have your special time – *then* you will matter. I was acutely aware of the jagged seams between work and life. Bringing your 'authentic self' to work i.e. that more soul-full you, does not ease the workload, nor does it mean that you are fully present. How can it be, if you find yourself dismissing the rest of you just to fit the corporate mould? Rest assured, those who love you in your life know the real story, they are the ones after all that make all of the allowances for your absences, whether physical or emotional because the reality is that with most corporate work there is simply not enough of you to go around and if you want to climb the ladder ever upward, you will have to give up more and more meaningful chunks of yourself and your home life to manage your increasing workload and, more importantly, show your true unswerving devotion to keep your place on the ladder. It's a choice you make even if you don't acknowledge this to yourself; it's our choice, after all, to do this – and *why?* The ego for one just loves it, loves your thirst-less quest for more – more money, more title, more visibility, more corporate need … she just wants you to keep going on that train as underneath it all she is driven be your primal fears like being homeless or having your kids go hungry, not fitting in, not having what every other Joe has … those fears ensure the ego always has your best survival interests at heart … or so she thinks.

So, the guilt and the grief were a roller-coaster that gained speed once I decided to sever the connection with my work life and team (this bounty of diverse souls within my neatly curated work community; together we would turn our hands to all manner of creation). To turn around and tell them that I was leaving them felt quite frankly like an ultimate act of betrayal, like a parent walking out on their family. Once I had taken the bold step to tell my manager of my impending departure, I decided to tell the team straight away so they wouldn't hear any miscommunication from anyone else. This was my stage right and I was the one that had to serve it and deal with the fall out. Their kind words of appreciation and the acknowledgment that I had done a good job as their manager and led our group well made for a tearful goodbye.

This act of separation was heartfelt and sorrowful, which made it very, very hard to let go.

Terror

So, with the severing of my identity, my connections, my daily routine, I was faced with a blankness that struck me with cold, uncompromising terror – after a life of always having to be somewhere and doing something, with its own cadence and the tools well honed to manage it, I had absolutely no idea of what I was going to *do* next. I simply knew two things – I could not go back now and I did not want to jump into something that was ultimately going to be the same, even though my ego tried so hard to press me toward even more exciting roles that agents would call me about daily. I had to basically switch it all off if I was going to get through this thing, whatever it was. I was going to have to STOP everything that was part of that old way of being, all of those interruptions and little hooks back into what was now my past life. But what in hell was I going to DO? The doing that had kept my every waking minute preoccupied for decades just stopped and in its place there seemed to be nothing ... this is where the terror lay in wait, a screaming black hole inside me that seemed to grow daily as my ego kept asking: *What are you going to do now? You have to DO something! What's next – you usually have a next? What's next and you better get it right, no room for mistakes now! You are essentially penniless, remember. You have everything riding on this next move so don't mess it up!*

The terror was all consuming because the DOING was no longer being done! I had no clear path, I just had an emptiness where my work life used to be, and now it felt like I was left with a barren piece of land, devoid of any structure or form to guide me. I felt incredibly alone, having told none of my friends or family, bar my partner whom I didn't want to overburden on top of everything else. The loneliness terrified me, not having any coherent thoughts about where to turn next terrified me, and not being able to share it with my family and friends just made me more and more isolated to a point where I felt like I was paralysed; literally both my body and my head had been stopped – stuck through a lack of doing – and I didn't know what to do about it! It almost felt like a type of madness, to be honest; I mean, here I was at 50 having decided to jack it all in and replacing it with nothing? Like in my favourite childhood movie, *The NeverEnding Story*, where the Nothing comes to vanquish everything, leaving a desert of dank, stark nothingness behind it … this is where I felt I was now, in a deep cavern submerged by the weight of a decision of my very own making.

This was not just about not going back to a job, it was about saying goodbye to a way of being I had known for well over half my life. It involved stepping outside my very existence to a place beyond myself that felt, for all intents and purposes, like I was hanging onto the edge of the world, just hanging by a thread with my ego up in arms, shaming and mocking me to try and cajole a way forward, any move, really. So I decided finally to sign up for something, a course that might keep me preoccupied so that the Nothing would disappear and yes, for a while the idea of doing 'the course' held me together, gave me a sense of direction. I was going to be DOING something soon and I would have something to tell people who came asking. I wouldn't have to feel like I had no story. This would make sense to them *and* to my ego; she loved it. *Yes, finally you have your next thing to do, your story almost sounds cohesive, you left that to do this, 'they' will buy that.* Yet I did have a concern – was I just replacing one form of *doing* with another, usurping all the time I had fought so hard to free up, now fully tied up and offered to yet another external entity again? Did it not just amount to the same thing? I would still end up with less of me to go around. What would I be achieving by doing this? Was it answering the need in me, and the terror again in making the wrong choice, creating the wrong outcome?

Rage

When I eventually wrangled the terror to a manageable state, another far more visceral emotion surfaced and she was angry; pure visceral white-hot rage poured forth, all aimed squarely at everyone around me for letting this happen, the corporate world's failure to harness my unique blend of talents – how could they just let me go? Was I not missed or indispensable? How would the business function without me? Apparently not, given no follow-up calls from corporate HR or the senior network to ask if I might consider going back. Now it was pure cold rejection that I was feeling on top of being appalled at how in denial I actually was about everything. Why was I longing to go back anywhere? The writing, when I stopped to think about it, had been on the wall for many years; I had just not wanted to see it and as I read my diaries up to ten years prior they echoed in unison the same voice, the same need, the same desire to break free – I had simply chosen to ignore it all and take what seemed the easier path, and thus this rage had been building and building. My soul was not satisfied to just hint at a new future – it wanted me to understand *why* so I wouldn't do a U-turn on myself as I had previously (albeit for crippling monetary need).

I was apt to point a guilty finger at any unsuspecting human that came within forty feet. The simplest thing could trigger a gush of molten rage so severe my partner and kids started to cower when I entered a room; needless to say, the road rage took the brunt as did the doors which were a joy to slam, letting out the pent-up energy which was continuously fizzing up inside me. I developed acute indigestion to the point where I couldn't keep anything down and I ended up just living on indigestion remedies for a few weeks. My hair seemed to stand on end, a frisson running through its ends and all the while I was simmering with a rage till eventually it reached boiling point and I was faced with either a body slam of such intensity I would never physically recover or I step up and simply deal with this outpouring, listen to what was being said. At this point I mercifully fell upon my copy of the book *The Artist's Way* by Julia Cameron, which encouraged me to revisit something that I had practised many moons ago … her 'morning pages'. Once I started writing them, I just tore those pages up with my pen each morning on rising. Chucking it all onto the page meant I wasn't carrying it around with me like some dark attachment all day and I found once it was out there on the page, I could breathe, I could focus, I had moments of actual clarity and I even started to enjoy my 'free' time.

Of course, I was obsessed with money at this point; how could I actually make things work if I wasn't going to let myself take the first job out there? I was going to have to figure out pretty fast how I could make ends meet for at least the immediate future. I had kids still in school, a fairly hefty mortgage and meagre savings so the weight of things really rested heavily day and night. The rage was a way of getting me to activate in a way; anger is an active state and from it you can really get a lot done. Those morning pages (God bless you, Julia Cameron) would find me a way out of this quagmire of my own making.

Acceptance

Forgiving myself for choosing the road less taken was an important step that I would revisit over and over again, particularly when my ego was having a recurring meltdown. Forgiveness and acceptance for the way things are right now in your life go hand in hand. When we accept ourselves as we truly are, in complete naked honesty, we let go our fears, pretensions and ego-driven belief systems that hold us back and keep us at a lower energy vibration that is misaligned with our soul's intent. The soul strives for unanimous harmony between body, mind and soul. When we let go of our desires and just accept who we are right at this very moment, we feel our real spiritual power, more powerful than any quick hit of the ego's fulfilment, more than anything anyone can give us. We simply grant ourselves the ultimate gift of freedom from these tyrannies, wants, needs ... By letting go, we give ourselves permission to accept our current situation with grace. We let go and the spirit steps in to support and guide us from a place of unconditional love. There is no precondition or criteria for receiving this limitless well of goodness; simply by yielding to it we can accept our very moment in this universe without fear or judgment, and by accepting ourselves completely without question we honour our own truth. So, I decided to forgive myself and accept my new destiny which in turn allowed me to (dare I say it) feel the tiniest bit excited about what was yet to come.

Working out my needs

Finally, I connected with a career coach to guide me with my new career approach, to ensure it aligned with my new needs. She agreed that part-time or contract work would be good for my current state of being and tasked me with taking some time first to work out what I actually enjoyed doing. It was at this point that I started to create a simple inventory of my life abilities, which essentially lumped together life skills by my enthusiasm for doing them, e.g. 'Love doing this', 'Would like to do more of that', 'Hate doing this' and 'Do not want to do it even if I was on my last crumb' and everything in between (see *Appendix: A Life Skills Matrix*). Then she helped pull apart the onion to aid me in identifying the type of roles that would most satisfy the need without 'selling my soul'. Most tellingly, she told me to focus on the fact that my next job would be just that: just a *next* job, not a forever job or anything that felt like it might hold me in thrall again. This time it would be me calling the shots on what suited my needs. So, if it was only three hours every afternoon bar Fridays then that was the fit we would look at addressing. There was absolutely nothing left off the table; this was a completely free space to help me understand what level of doing I could actually cope with, without feeling that my core had been compromised. I was fairly clear that that breach could not and would not ever happen in my life again.

CHAPTER 5

Stepping Back

Maybe Maslow had it right?

To step back and try to figure out if I was in the midst of a midlife breakdown (probably), I decided to refer to the experts on what we need as humans to be happy. Starting with Maslow's well-loved hierarchy of needs (see below), we can quickly determine the motivating factors that drive our current decision-making and, as a result, the very course of our lives:

Self Actualisation
Being the best version of yourself

Esteem
Respect, strength, status, freedom, recognition

Love & belonging
Family, friends, intimacy, community

Safety needs
Security, health, resources, work property

Physiological needs
Air, water, food, sleep, clothing, shelter

Starting at the bottom of the triangle, if you are struggling to keep a roof over your head and food on the table, then this is going to be your overarching driver and the higher planes of receiving respect and reaching your absolute life actualisation are not going to seem that pertinent. You need to make sure you can square the financials with making sure your basic biological needs are met, along with building up your safety net once an opportunity presents itself to do so, e.g. paying a ridiculously high rent or mortgage that meets or exceeds your income, making it impossible for you to consider anything else but balancing the book each week. This is where you need to focus your energy right now, e.g. by moving to a cheaper location, downsizing, moving in with parents … whatever will allow you to meet your basic needs and also offer you the potential to move on to the next step, in other words, build your safety net. After your basic needs and safety are secured, then it is possible to focus on building further connections, whether they be with family, friends, a new lover … Reaching out beyond your current place in the world now you are safe and fed, feels like a natural next step. This could be joining a local community group, helping family members or volunteering, all of which expand our feeling of connectedness with life.

After that, you are either looking for outward esteem in the form of formal recognition or validation by society, your community or friends etc, and inward esteem by working on how you feel about yourself, your needs, your confidence, and how you value yourself (I think this is a life-long exercise that we hone as we continue to grow, getting to know ourselves more deeply with the growing of wisdom along with grey hair!)

The final step at fulfilling your life's needs, that pinnacle of self-actualisation by reaching the top of the pyramid and of your life, is different in reality for everyone as it depends on what you feel your true life journey means to you, and what it should entail for you to feel fulfilled and successful.

Reflection

When I tried to pin down which of these areas I recognised most as a need for myself, I could say in truth that a piece of all of them applied as I ricocheted between stages. I certainly was trying to ensure all my family's basic needs could be met after quitting corporate life (see Chapter 7 Doing the Math) whilst I was trying to figure out what made me feel secure as I worked out my thresholds for safety, e.g. someone who is really wealthy could stack a wad of money in savings every month for their rainy day fund, I in contrast would put by a small amount of rainy day money into the credit union which equally made me feel secure knowing if everything fell apart I would have some 'get out of jail' money that I could fall back on. At the same time, I was reaching out to friends, now realising that my support network was invaluable for having fun, just letting off steam sometimes or pushing me forward on my journey when I became bogged down. Beyond that, the need to be a part of broader groups such as my running club, the innovation lab to exchange ideas or volunteering all helped to ensure I could continue to broaden my horizon and keep moving forward. Even though my heart's desire was self-actualisation, uncovering my true path and learning all the skills I needed to reach my inner potential, I felt my overarching need resonated most with self-esteem. Taking a deeper look here, putting words to the uncomfortable emotions, allowed me to acknowledge that I lacked self-belief in my own abilities. I literally laughed at myself for having the nerve to think I could actually have it all; *who does she think she is?* Oh, I could hear my ego's disdain … the quieter soul voice pulled me closer and whispered, '*Love who you are right now at this very moment; there are no conditions for love, just love that person inside you no matter what and with all of your being.*' From this acorn, self-belief and validation and trust grew.

Task

Looking at Maslow's hierarchy of needs, which do you feel you resonate with the most right now? What are you looking for here or what do you feel you need? What steps do you need to take to meet that need?

Digging deeper into the steps of transformation

Looking at the emotional heave-ho I had been experiencing and in the process of stepping back, I realised I was not alone in my reactions; it turns out that making life-changing decisions propels one into a cycle of transformation whether we are open to it or not. Looking at the broad series of speakers on coping with change, I concluded the set of steps below reflected the journey I had been on once I decided I needed to leave corporate life for my own well-being.

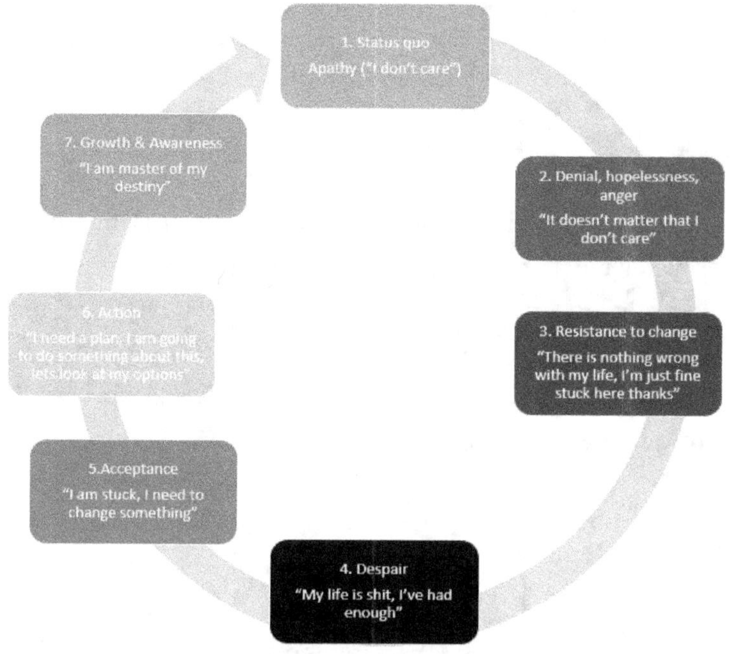

STEP 1: Status quo

The first step in everyone's journey is where you find yourself right now: your status quo.

If you feel you have become apathetic about what you are doing, why you are doing it and who you are doing it with, or you feel it even deeper in your bones like a numbness or mental disengagement, even at your worst having a sense of disembodiment, then you, my friend are silently champing away at the entry gate to transformation, you just haven't recognised it in yourself yet. The body knows what it needs so it starts to tell you in subtle ways that all is not well with your world, and you fail to feel the adrenaline or any real sign of positive emotion towards where you are in your life right; now you move to step 2.

STEP 2: Denial

When you are actively digging into your status quo whilst deeply feeling the apathy and numbness and replying, 'I'm fine, really' to anyone who deigns to ask if you are really alright, then you are on the precipice of denial. Not wanting to rock the boat or daring to even consider any upset to the status quo are common responses.

STEP 3: Resistance to Change

Digging in even further, when you find you are downright appalled or angry even, that anyone might suggest that you should look at changing such-and-such to alleviate some of the clear discontent starting to seep from your core, then you are deep in the trenches of your own resistance. This is at its heart a form of defence. Not wanting to create any change that might rock the boat in your corporate life, you start to retreat from anything that might seem like it is in direct conflict to the safe rut you have found yourself in. Your rut, I'm sure, is really rather cosy, fettered from years of giving up pieces of your soul in exchange for corporate goodies like climbing the ladder, getting more visibility across the organisation, more money, more ego boosts. But this in and of itself is actual regression from the very life you were born to live, and is counter to your growth as a human.

STEP 4: Despair

Allowing step 3 to continue for a long time will eventually lead to step 4, because the body knows that change is the only true life constant and trying to shield oneself from it is akin to dying while still alive. This brings forth the feelings of hopelessness, that somehow you have become disconnected from some out of reach mystical part of your being that has been lost or exchanged for 'corporate betterment'.

Despair can only go one of two ways and it may be high time to consider a corp*exit* – kicking that despair into touch, you fight back as if you're life depended on it (it does).

STEP 5: Acceptance

If by some sheer moment of frustration or anger or clinging to the brink of despair you realise that this is a problem and it needs to be addressed, then you have just taken the first upward step towards a more positive way of living. Even if you can't or don't want to acknowledge that part, just acknowledging the problem will start to free you from the tyranny of apathy that has ruled you and quashed any potential for growth with it.

Well done you if you have got to this step; keep going. It will be worth it, I assure you!

STEP 6: Action

Deciding you want to take action is an incredible gift to yourself. By the very act of deciding this, you already start to undo the shackle that has held you back and ready yourself to push through, up and out of the corporate bubble. So get a basic plan of action together, write down the steps you need to follow to exit gracefully (read the other chapters to build your awareness of the areas you should consider but don't get bogged down!). The most important thing at this point is to build your plan, commit to it and start to action it; that first step is all it takes for your transformation to kick off. Remember to diarise this journey as it will amaze you to see how far you've come.

STEP 7: Growth and Awareness

Welcome to the promised land – your journey of transformation will be rewarded with a more acute awareness of what your life-path entails and where you need and want to spend your time and energy going forward to be truly happy.

Task

Where do you feel you currently are on the cycle of transformation? Note that even if you are still considering getting off the starting block, at least you are there challenging yourself to what may come next!

CHAPTER 6

Assembling a Tool-box

Finally, I had to call time on the emotional roller-coaster and start to put a shape on things to make sense of it all, given that I seemed to lack a set of tools for dealing with this unyielding web of emotion that was trapping my essence to the point of paralysis. What could I do to allow myself to see things from another angle and assist me to move forward? I called to the chair both my ego and my soul for my very first life SOS brainstorming session, and from this my tool-box was born, a set of life-enabling supports that helped me move from stuck to a more liberated state where I could start to visualise a whole new future.

Getting fit

My toolbox started unwittingly by signing up to a 28-day fitness challenge at a local gym, simply to shift all the weight I had put on during the pandemic. Of course, I didn't quite achieve that but what I did do was give myself an opportunity to improve my physical wellness which in turn improved my mental wellness. The stress I had been absorbing from work found a way to slowly peter away and with that released a far more upbeat energy which replaced it. In fact, it was this that became infectious to me during my 28 days; the hormonal high, if you will, just treating myself in a positive way started to yield good vibes in many areas of my life. I was no longer just sitting on the couch, hand-to-mouth ingesting sugar and carbs the way I had been for over two years now without editing any of it. My desire to actually *do* things came back like an old friend. It had been away for a long, long time and if felt so good to want to do something other than just work. Just opening the door to myself was enough for that magical quality of 'flow' (everything running smoothly with no intervention where often coincidental things happened) to enter my life once again.

Meditating

It had been a very long time since I allowed myself the few quiet moments it took to reconnect with my inner self; just five minutes a day sitting in a chair by the window had a profoundly calming effect. I had forgotten how good it feels to simply clear the clutter of an overworked mind. I would literally visualise myself turning the dial from high to low, then to off with a click to help mute that mind voice which was hoarse from being in overdrive all those years. In this cornered-off time, I was giving it all a rest, just letting the energy flow as needed, all the while purely focusing on my breath. In and out, in and out, gently visualising my feet connecting deep into the earth like roots looking for moisture from the ground, sand between my toes while at the same time feeling a silver cord flow from the top of my mind upward to the sky, just breathing in a soft pink feeling of love that lives in abundance all around us and allowing it to flow down through me into the ground. I focused on nurturing all those dark interior corners harbouring my worries and fears, those tight little spaces and balled-up fists which were stopping me really breathing in life. Meditating offered me a quiet inner sanctuary, and this quietness in turn allowed my subconscious freedom to share any immediate insights or needs that might help me at that time. Literally five minutes and my mind was calm, my body felt soft, warmed and rested, my intuition and clarity sharpening with every breath.

Morning journaling

As I mentioned earlier, I started following Julia Cameron's *The Artist's Way*. each week, initially starting what are called Morning Pages which is just writing down whatever junk enters your head on waking each day for two-three pages without judging or editing it. It is a pure stream of consciousness which de-junks the mind and it helps to build a link with your subconscious once you start to do it each day. I found this wonderfully cathartic, having last given it a go in my 20s when I was backpacking. I certainly now had far more junk off-loading each day and I started to enjoy the lighter feeling it gave me. My mind, free of worries and fears, calmed itself down as I fell into the discipline of doing this, though of course there were days when I missed doing this as things inevitably cropped up in life, but each time I would steer myself right back to doing the pages each day, but never ever reading them … just letting it all hang out, letting it all be.

After a few weeks, I can honestly say I felt the power of flow re-entering my life. I was starting to enjoy very simple things again like going for a walk and seeing nature in its glory in the most mundane places; it felt as if a well were forming deep below, a clear pool of cool water amassing inside of me, helping to clarify and purify my inner life. Each week I set myself a chapter of Julia's book to work through and faithfully carried out each of the tasks she prescribed, without judgment … somehow I knew that I needed to do this, it was all part of the exhumation of my spiritual self, like a phoenix from the flames just when I thought I had well and truly died inside; this humble set of activities revived me and helped me to trust myself again.

I had been trusting work with my direction for a very long time, but there can only be one captain of your ship and that, my friend, is not the corporate life but *your* life. No matter how important your corporate work might make us feel or how necessary we may think it is for us to succeed in life, devoting all of your waking hours to your exterior life without any to your interior life vanquishes any opportunity you may have for intuition and really hearing your own self and what you need.

We need to stop looking for this from others, searching apps, looking for signs – our life compass is buried deep within us and only needs us to set some time aside to tune in. If we fail to do this, then we blindly follow the compass of others, whether it's the corporate's, or your family's and friends', and here is where your dissonance will set in as you move off-course to follow the direction of another without fully understanding what *you* need to survive.

Cooking and the sharing of food

As a way of bringing myself to a state of well-being, I started to take an interest in cooking again. This was not the military operation I had attacked frantically during my work breaks to be ready for when the kids came home from school – this cooking involved allowing myself time every once in a while to idly pour over a recipe book then go the local market to buy whatever I fancied on that given day so I could conjure up whatever feast seemed appropriate for the day. This felt like such a gift, and the sheer joy of cooking coupled with the desire to share my latest bounty with whomever crossed our threshold was a thrill. Cooking is such a natural way to connect with other human beings and I had almost forgotten the joy it brings; it does not have to be the fancy affair of *Masterchef*, striving for unattainable perfection; instead, these creative bursts were humble, fun, messy affairs that served to share an energy and life moments with others and giving you the opportunity to listen, really listen for once to your guests in return. It was a simple pleasure that opened a door out of the isolation chamber I had found myself in, where life had become overwhelmingly busy and which in turn blocked any chance of taking on a messy creative task without aspiring to the corporate ideal of perfection or other people's vision of what the perfect meal should be. Cooking was simply using whatever was there on the day, no judgment with the outcome, nourishing my soul and those souls around me.

Self-care

Small moments of self-care dotted through the week created a daisy-chain of loveliness that really buoyed me up when I was up and down, whether it was a bath filled with a handful of Epsom salts or some gifted bath bomb, the lighting of a scented candle, the gathering of flowers from a nearby field, the bubble of the humidifier filled with a few drops of essential oils, the glow of a salt lamp and a soft woollen blanket whilst reading or listening to a book, a mug of coffee in a café on a rainy day, a walk through the wood in wellies, a dash along the beach with the dog …These moments of self-care felt cherished, encasing myself in a loving bubble as I transitioned from a fragile shell of being to a more robust, fleshed-out human being. As I began to unravel, I understood that the best thing I could do for myself was to show myself kindness, unjudged little luxuries that cost almost nothing but brought a feeling of care at a time when I felt incredibly vulnerable and unable to ask others for help. Even changing my clothing from the stylized harsh contours and colours of the corporate uniform to softer, more organic textures, enveloping myself with whatever colour I felt I needed on a given day would mean a lot. Sometimes I might be in bright mustard yellow from head to toe on a very grey day, verdant purples, the purifying sanctity of white, or I'd envelope myself in black when I felt like I really needed to switch off and don my cloak of invisibility.

I listened gently during my meditation to what was needed and tended to it as I would lovingly tend to someone I truly cared for, only this time the person receiving the benefit was me.

Tasks

What relaxes you and helps you to unwind (beyond the odd glass of wine!); how often do you afford yourself the time to take pleasure in doing the things you love? Do you think you could make a date with yourself on a regular basis, to take that time for just your own enjoyment (even if it's an hour a week, it will be an hour that is yours, a true gift to yourself to acknowledge that yes, you are special, and yes, you *do* deserve this).

CHAPTER 7

Doing the Math

To figure out if my family could afford all of this impending change, I sat down and worked things out as if I was doing the yearly budgets in work, the sources of income and all the outgoings so I had a clear understanding of the total ask each month. Next, I set about prioritising the must-haves over the nice-to-haves so I could identify areas ripe for cuts.

The mortgage – did we need to move? I was not ready to make such a big decision from the outset so decided first to see what options I had in terms of trying to sustain the current mortgage for a while at least. So, I reviewed the latest rates across all lenders to see how we could bag ourselves a more competitive rate by switching. It turns out that all the home insulating we had invested in over the years adds up to a decent enough home energy rating which, once certified, meant I could apply for a home improvements mortgage rate, the lowest on the market. This was a first move, along with reducing the payment and extending it over as long a term as possible to lock in a monthly mortgage repayment that we could cover if we had to rent the property, if worst came to worst.

Turning 50 meant I could take some advantage of the post-50 early retirement payouts from my pension (specifically, accessing 25% of some of the small pension pots I had paid into over the years, though the larger corporate-based funds remained inaccessible until I reached at least 60). So, liberating some money from these small pots could help keep things ticking over for a while until I figured out a more robust model. I set about doing all the paperwork and, let me tell you, there is a lot! It became my daily admin for a while.

Checking out any tax back owed was my next move; it turns out there are lots of vendors willing to help you do this for a small fee for each year you process and I could go back five years. At first it seemed I would actually owe more than I received back but then all those corporate health insurance contributions actually helped with unclaimed tax relief so I made a tidy saving here overall.

Next, I started to look at immediate ways I could start to deliver an income to the household given the impending bills, and I happened upon the idea of taking in a student. The guest room that I had been holding spare for the guests who rarely visited got a quick lick of paint, new curtains, bedding and recycled furniture and was placed on a room rental site. We received a request for a room literally the same day as we placed it, so we decided to give it a try, knowing full well that our teens would not be happy and we ourselves were nervous about having a stranger in our midst. It turned out to be a very good experience: our first student arrived the next day and tucked herself in as if she had always been there. Of course, the teens were up in arms, sharing the bathroom with a stranger, never mind sharing the kitchen and actually having to say hello when they entered the room, plus not screaming the house down when they felt like it! It was all too much to bear for them so they retreated. My partner and I welcomed the peace and this new person, young, energetic and outgoing with her own social scene, was a breath of fresh air, and the money, of course, helped to alleviate some of the impending financial worry.

I next did a hatchet job on all inconsequential outgoings such as magazine subscriptions, newspapers, music subscriptions, gaming subscriptions. Yes, they all went and not without significant wailing, I can tell you. We set new expectations on the handouts which had just become obscene and, quite frankly, potentially destructive if left unchecked for much longer. I paid off the car loan, got rid of the credit card and the overdraft from the pension pots so we ended up with a streamlined list of bills that made the cut. Any must-have items the teens demanded would need to wait till Christmas or birthdays but either way our expenses were going down.

Confronted with a collapsed income and still the same outgoings and life expectations, I understood quite quickly that things were going to have to change. Yes, I could initially plug the gaps with money from my savings / pension release but that was not something that would regenerate or be sustainable over time. So, changing how we approached things was a necessary action, a difficult task when I was not a fan of repressed spending – quite the opposite, in fact. When my pay cheque arrived each month, after paying the stack of ongoing bills, I would always relish spending whatever was left on dining out, throwing money at the kids, buying clothes, household goods, gifts and so on, without a second thought. I felt I had earned the splurge after toiling the previous month. This way of being had to transform along with everything else. These are the things I considered:

- Reducing holidays abroad and buying flights and accommodation well in advance whilst shopping around for the best deals. Setting a budget for this was essential as it is too easy to get caught up in the need for that one week away which goes very fast and then you have 51 weeks ahead of you, so I needed to look at alternative opportunities for taking a break. Enter the camper … you can imagine how that went down with the teens! A total non-runner. I decided on a vintage camper that wouldn't clean me out of savings but would offer a means of escape when needed and should the teens ever decide they wanted to join us (which was looking less and less likely with every passing year anyway!). Worst case scenario, they could pitch up a tent beside the van. As I say, this idea did not go down well with them but it has provided a salvatory means of escape when needed for the adults in the household – a real life-sustaining benefit!

- Stopping my gym membership was hard to do. I had built up a nice community of friends on the two days a week I went to the gym but justifying the heavy monthly subscription became impossible, especially when I had decided to take up running which was essentially free. Initially starting with the couch-to-5k, I signed myself up for the women's mini marathon, a 10km race that would give me something to aim towards. Once that race had passed, I signed up for my next milestone: a half-marathon. With my move to running, whilst the gym certainly complimented my training, I could not justify the spend so I joined a local running club which provided an alternative community to connect with each week, also assisting with interval training to help build up my stamina. I decided to invest in a second-hand bench and weights (to continue building up the muscles I had started to develop from the gym and which could be used by others in the household), creating an opportunity to share an interest in fitness in the house was a very unexpected but welcome benefit.

- Going out for slap-up meals and the endless stream of take-aways (because I was often too tired to cook after a 10-hour day) was next in the firing line. Not only had I a tyre of stomach weight to work on losing, it was a growing monthly cost with potential health-impacting hazards that we were in need of addressing. Developing an interest in cooking again (now that I had the time) was a joy I had long forgotten and eager to develop in my young cohort (cooking each day to a set timetable becomes a real monotony that needs to be shared), as well as developing necessary life skills they would need once they fled the nest. It also helped reduce the outgoings, whilst also reducing the roll of fat I was carrying around.

- In a similar vein, going out for drinks was pared back, and instead we invited friends over for 'a cocktail in the van', a walk with coffee or the odd barbecue, a much more sustainable approach to socialising while addressing a growing alcohol dependency I had been fostering as a 'stress-reliever'. Clearly I had not computed that alcohol was a depressant more often than not, contributing to my stressed state.

- Buying clothes and getting my hair and nails done was a

particularly challenging personal sacrifice but again one I acknowledge as a significant outgoing when reviewing my monthly bank statement. The truth was I had enough clothes and while I could colour my hair myself and paint my own nails and get a haircut in cheaper salons up to twice a year, it was the pampering aspect that I really missed. So, allowing myself an isolated clothes purchase every now and then in a non-boutique space where I would spend a lot less became a planned for treat that I could look forward to, rather than the blind monthly retail splurge it had become. For each new piece, I now stopped to consider what I could let go of in return as wardrobe space was at a premium, and the act of cleansing the wardrobe was cathartic and an unexpected bonus.

- We got rid of the second car and decided not to upgrade our current model that was still going well. Instead, we looked after it better and moved to using bicycles alongside advocating the of use of public transport, in particular for the teens who had become very used to the Mummy/Daddy taxi service, making us all more self-sufficient whilst lightening our CO^2 load and making us leaner.

- Now that I did not have the corporate covering our medical cover, the private medical insurance costs were beyond what we could afford. It was true that we were all becoming healthier so the key thing to have money for would be in the event of accidents / unforeseen medical emergencies. Yes, we would be at the mercy of the public health system but we decided that this was a necessary step, and if really needed, we decided it would be preferable to pay for a procedure in a private hospital if the waiting list in public was long. Better than paying the hefty annual fee for something covering only the *possibility* of something happening.

- Likewise, travel insurance was no longer seen as a necessity; if flights were cancelled, they were often either covered by the airline themselves, depending on the reason for cancellation, or cheap enough to be rebooked. Given we were only traveling once a year, this was not a huge saving by any means.

- We looked into the benefit of getting solar panels and a heat pump versus paying the growing energy bills, but for now could not make such an investment, especially as the return would be over a much longer period. So we decided we would continue to review newer options as they become available to see if a more readily available cost-benefit return could be achieved. Instead, we focused on reducing what we could – turning off heating for at least six months of the year, apart from half an hour each morning for showers, reducing the areas where electricity was really needed, turning off switches, and moving to more energy efficient ways of doing things, e.g. letting laundry dry naturally on the clothesline rather than using the dryer, moving to an air-fryer, George Foreman grill or barbecuing instead of heating the entire grill/oven; all of these helped. Most significantly, investing in attic insulation paid dividends in less heat loss.

- Our pets also came under review: we changed their food to bigger and less specialised packets and fed them our meat and fish leftovers, so nothing went to waste. We also bought their worming and flea treatments in bigger quantities at the supermarket rather than through the vets and stopped the pet insurance which had never been used anyway, and again, we would cover the vet bills if and when needed.

- We reviewed our collective music subscriptions, newspaper delivery, Xbox and other gaming membership, audible and such like, which helped us to focus on what we could share. We replaced our audio book services with the free library app, for example, where you can order books online for collection at your local library or remove the subscription altogether and ask the household to prioritise to work within a collective budget.

- Gifting took a hit also as we realised we could no longer afford the big fancy presents for Christmas time extended family gatherings. Instead, I gave thoughtful consideration to family or individual based gifts that might offer a pleasurable experience rather than a visual material impact such as family tickets for a day out at a pet farm (rather than each family member getting their own big gift), a lunchtime theatre show at a fraction of the cost of a night time show, little home-made hampers (food/spa/hobbies etc) made from carefully selected items suited to the needs of the giftee. Really considering the interest of each giftee became more central to the gifting process than the amount of money I could throw at it due to a previous lack of time and energy, thus resulting in a far more genuine and heartfelt approach.

As well as reducing our spend, we focused on the need to continue saving a little and often in our local credit union. Just a small amount saved over the year becomes enough to cover next year's holiday, any unplanned medical expenses or life events. Getting our teens to think in the same way as they pocketed money from their casual work would, I felt, help them save more enthusiastically over the course of their lives.

Reflection

As part of the change in your status, you will find yourself confronted with the need to make certain lifestyle sacrifices and some thought should be given to what you are willing to compromise on and what you are not. You will also find that work-related opportunities and diversions are thrown into your path in a way to test you. Before jumping to the next thing, it is really important to take time to identify what you really need to cover your basic needs so you have clarity on your bottom-line. Also, question what conditioning is at play if you feel you are obligated or duty-bound to do work if it feels in conflict with your genuine heart's desire.

Sometimes we genuinely cannot turn down an offer of work because of the basic needs that need to be met but if you have a choice on how to shape that work so that it still lets your soul breathe or alters your course so that you find the right fit so you and yours can sleep peacefully at night, then do what you can to find that balance for yourself.

Task

What are your non-compromisable lifestyle priorities? What could you learn to do without? Is there an opportunity for changing your lifestyle to a more optimal model that better serves your needs longer term? What might that optimal life model look like for you? What steps would you need to take to start moving towards that new way of living? What benefits do you think might come from the change?

CHAPTER 8

Family Impact

It is a gross underestimation to say that my children were unhappy with this new change in their lives. As typical teenagers, their concerns lay centred around my ability to meet their needs on an ongoing basis, coupled with a desire to still be part of their tribe. So, my sharing with them that I had left the corporate fold did not go down at all well. In fact, it has been a bone of contention ever since. The fact that I now no longer hold a corporate job title or a corporate pay cheque is seen by my children as the single most ridiculous decision ever to be made as it displaces them from their footing in the tribe where parents are expected to diligently go out to work each day to a job of sufficient status to demand the admiration of those around them; breaking rank was akin to a treacherous act similar to a soldier running away from a war that they no longer wanted to be a part of.

The real concern of course was how their financial needs where going to be met going forward; it appeared that there was no way I could source an income by doing things a different way. No, these shareholders wanted to ensure their bottom-line would be met on an ongoing basis and how was I going to do that without a consistent pay cheque coming in?

They were not interested, rather they were fully disgusted by the idea that I may look for income by a) renting a room out to students, b) part-time work, c) unlocking my pension. Their horror at this new situation ran very deep; they could not look at me without feeling that I had indeed done them a huge disservice, even though I was continuing to put food on the table, drip-feeding them endless tenners, paying their school fees and taking them on holiday to boot. Still, I remained in the laser focus of their derision. 'When are you going to get a proper job?' 'You are such an embarrassment', 'Please go back to work' became the pining chorus each morning as I drove them to school.

I felt sorry for them in a way, not being able to see that life transformation does come at a price and their need for security and stability was, I admit, being threatened by me so they had a legitimate right to moan. I just did not consider that it would go on for so long or take such a venomous course. Regardless of what I did, it never seemed enough until eventually I decided it was high-time they started to consider how they could make a small income to sustain themselves. I had ongoing babysitting jobs during my teens, a job that seemed a no-brainer but they just wanted to continue the life of idle abandon they felt was their due. When I broached the subject of them getting a job, I received the replies that school had categorically said it would be a bad idea to get jobs lest it interfere with schoolwork, but given this was summer, I failed to see where the conflict lay.

I remained committed to my course of action, understanding that their young minds would eventually come round, and meanwhile there was nothing much I could do to shelter them from the reality that life *does* change and sometimes there are circumstances beyond their control that they need to deal with. Resilience was to be the lesson of the year for us all, and developing new coping skills could only benefit our family life in the long run, as long as I could keep the wolf from the door.

Reflection

The adage that to make an omelette you have to break a few eggs certainly applies here. The reality is that leaving the safety of the corporate space will have a perceptible impact on those around you as they revalue your place and consequently theirs (if part of your immediate cohort) as a result of your repositioning in their social hierarchy.

Task

How do you think your nearest and dearest will react to your change of course? What ways will it specifically impact them and what would your response be to those impacts? Is there an opportunity for growth and change in your family circle as a result of your action? How might it benefit you all in the long run?

CHAPTER 9

Understanding *why* we work

All the pressure of finding a job ASAP so that I could work and be a worker and thus not feel like I had become exiled from the other 99% of humans on the planet now came with a deep inner conflict for me as I knew that any 'work' would simply take time away from my new soul-seeking adventure. In fact, work would act in direct conflict to what I wanted to achieve for myself rather than being the beneficiary we make it out to be in our lives through the provision of material things that make us feel secure.

Of course, everyone needs to be able to put a roof over their head and food on the table: these are basic human needs, but the question I had begun to ask myself was if I could manage to meet those absolute basic needs by simplifying my family's life to such a degree that we could get by whilst enabling me to continue on my quest, then why should I feel guilty about not working? I realised it was not working that most of all had me in a spiral of guilt which resulted in me looking for jobs then repelling them last minute when I felt they would effectively kill off my creative shoots. This conditioning was not apt to let me go that easily, for the need to work is sewn deep down into our DNA; it is what we expect of ourselves and what society expects of us. At this point I considered the challenge of our need for security over our need to find our soul's expression, which ultimately was more important for us in the long run. We could keep on living under the illusion that the job we did 80% of our lives was meaningful because it feeds us, clothes us, lets us go on the family vacation, lets us keep up with the Jones, but are we all part of one big delusion? What if we could whittle down that percentage to meet our basic needs, thereby giving ourselves the gift of time to really live? What might we achieve for ourselves then?

I wonder if the financial elite in the world feels the same conditioning at play in their day to day lives? They certainly would not have the same basic needs to be met and thus they do already have the choice to find their soul expression – to be the person they were born to be (if they choose to do good in contrast with global dictators and political despots who choose to do bad at the worker's expense). I started to question if work was something that has been inflicted *on us*, like the guilt inherent in an overly religious upbringing, rather than our innate desire (it can be hard to tell the difference when we take just a cursory glance) so I decided to do some research.

Sergio Caredda in his book *Future of Work* looks at where work began. With the creation of a hierarchy of landowners, there came a need for people (including women and slaves) to carry out the physical work, so that this elite could concentrate on advancing humanity.

https://sergiocaredda.eu/people/future-of-work/part-1-a-brief-history-of-work/

Of course, our approach to work and its place in our lives has continued to evolve over time, but centuries of conditioning have left us with a deeply entrenched belief system that prizes work over our own freedom. There has always been this elite, a small handful of families at the pinnacle of financial wealth in the world, who not only have the luxury of not having to work or sell their time for a living but who also have had plenty of time over the centuries to steer the future of humanity as desired. It surely has to be to the elite's benefit that the rest of us are kept busy grafting for a living so they can get on with running our world in a way that best suits their own agenda, rather than meeting our broader human need.

An article from Jeremy Seabrook, of *The Guardian*, deep dives further into the darker etymology of the words 'work' or 'labour', unearthing their relationship with a type of coercion as he digs deep into their derivation in a variety of European languages. See here for details:

https://www.theguardian.com/commentisfree/2013/jan/14/language-labouring-reveals-tortured-roots1#:~:text=The%20English%20%22work%22%20has%20an,bear%20down%20upon%20or%20compel.

Whilst the majority of us associate a lack of work or unemployment with poverty, if our basic financial needs were met via a universal living wage, for example, then work may not be necessary for the human condition, rather creativity would be allowed to develop, unless you are one of the lucky few mortals who has already successfully married their creativity to generating an income! I doubt many in the corporate world could claim such luck, unless you are one of the very few real decision-makers right at the top of the organisation tree. For the rest of us, work is something we do simply because:

a. We believe that we really do like working.

b. We have to make ends meet.

c. We are socially conditioned to feel that we have to work to be successful humans.

d. We feel we are important doing something important when we work, so our ego feels fulfilled.

e. We don't know what else we would do if we did not work as we have never given ourselves the time to explore this option – for most of us it is a mixture of these.

f. We are one of the lucky few that may even reach Maslow's peak of self-actualisation – we are doing what our very soul aspires to do.

When we look to the future, AI is almost certainly going to play a bigger role in the way we view work and the opportunities to be found by looking at life alternatives presented by job automation, whether we like it or not. In my research, I came across a recently released documentary, *After Work**, by Helen Hester and Nick Srnicek, which helped me delve deeper here. This work looks at why, over centuries, humans have driven the work ethic and how we view ourselves through our work. Looking to the future, they share a vision about what it would mean for human society if work ceased to exist and how we would value our free time within this context.

So, if we did not work, we would not cease to exist; in fact, if our basic needs for food and housing are met and our aspirations alter to allow ourselves the freedom to consider who we are at our core and what we do with our life*time*, it could open up limitless possibilities for research and exploration to evolve our society and the human condition in a more meaningful way – as long as we are collectively in the humanity driver seat rather than the machines of an elite set of decision-makers!

Reflection

Considering work started as a form of servitude, so wealthy landowners could reap the benefits of a good harvest, it has transformed in terms of what humans do over the centuries, but the overall construct of working for someone in exchange for money or sustenance hasn't changed. We still need to generate income to live but we have a lot more choice in terms of how we do that today. Instead of working down a mine or at the coal-face of financial services, you can choose to setup your own business, work to help others, work as a vlogger, run your own farm or co-op, work for the state ... the options are thankfully more varied so we can choose – consciously – what would work best for ourselves.

Task

Think about what work means to you – does it offer you what you need? What would you choose to do if work as we know it ceased to exist?

CHAPTER 10

Leaving the Cult of Corporate

I was interested to discover in my reading on corporate culture that there is a growth in the understanding that cultish company culture is not only alive and thriving, in fact it appears to be carefully curated by a number of corporate entities so as to ensnare workers on all levels: emotional, psychological and physiological, just as it would in a cult.

Cult derives from the Latin word cultus meaning 'care, labour, cultivation, culture, worship, reverence', originating from 'tended, cultivated' which are the past participles of 'colere' meaning 'to till'

https://etymonline.com (Accessed: 10 August 2023)

Stop for a second and see if you can think of any companies off-hand which have any of the following cult characteristics:

- A charismatic leader or management team who like to think of themselves as being disruptors

- A cultural doctrine with its own ideology, branding and made-up words that are used every day

- A common way of dressing, corporate uniform or even casual wear bearing the corporate logo (sometimes worn on weekends)

- Encourage you to spend your social time on campus, playing pool, going to the gym, eating free food, going out after hours with your work crew
- Encourage you to think of your co-workers as family

A number of Silicon Valley companies spring to mind, but there are more right around you, albeit maybe less obvious and if you start to really think about it, especially those heavily focusing on the corporate culture and the way people think, you may note a few you had not expected. You may even be part of such an organisation!

My investigation on the subject led me to an insightful work by Dave Arnott, author of *Corporate Cults: The Insidious Lure of the All-Consuming Organisation*, which looks into the cult-like tactics used by some companies at the ultimate expense of the worker.[1]

------

[1] Arnott, D (1999) *Corporate Cults: The Insidious Lure of the All-Consuming Organisation*: AMACOM

Identifying the cultish characteristics one works with in a corporate and how to break free

Much in the same way as a cult member buys wholeheartedly into the ethos and cult belief of a system, an organisation can create a cult-like environment to better exercise control over its members. Here are some well known cult characteristics that do not look out of place in the corporate sphere we work in today:

Submission

When you start to invest unquestioning loyalty and trust in your organisation and leadership, your increased submission is often rewarded with additional responsibilities, status or even financial reward. Your corporate buy-in or submission not only increases the importance of the organisation in your life, grooming your ego in the corporate group, but also allows the corporate to gain more control of your thinking time, informing your belief systems and forming a lens of how you view the world around you and your place in it. Without even being conscious of it, you can start to become a corporate clone, and may passionately defend the organisation even above that of the family or the community you live in.

Exclusivity

'No organisation can compete with us', 'We are number one at …' The organisation is successful when its employees believe they are better off working for it rather than a competitor. The notion of corporate exclusivity blinkers the worker from realism or truths about the worker's own place in the world. Feeling you are part of an exclusive group that uses your own corporate centric jargon (even when down the pub!) can make you feel looked after, untouchable and even safe.

Control

Monitoring and correcting your behaviour to ensure it aligns with the organisation's values is routinely managed in corporate via the performance management system, often relying on a bell curve or 'forced ranking' approach to rank employees from top to bottom, as well as grouping the high performers (top 20% usually) alongside the middle performers (around 70%) and the bottom 10% or underperforming group that require action if they are to be allowed to stay within the organisation. Behavioural adjustment is required to either bring the worker into line or be routinely worked through until they must leave the organisation.

Isolation or Love Bombing

'Love bombing' is an attempt to influence a person by demonstrations of attention and affection. 'Psychologists have identified love-bombing as part of a cycle of abuse and have warned against it.' (Ref Wikipedia).

This is a particularly divisive tool used in organisations to influence the behaviour of someone in the group. It is often used at senior levels of the organisation where managers can find themselves either in the hallowed inner-circle or visibly isolated from it. As one submits more to the organisation, this tool in itself can foster emotional dependence on the senior team's ideology. Being seen to heavily buy-in and even brown-nose to achieve visibility and a sense of belonging, an employee can achieve 'favourite of the month' as they are moved along the corporate trajectory.

Indoctrination

Continual management meetings, corporate updates/bulletins and ongoing 'training', as well as continuous organisational directives all serve as the means to get employees on board with the company's doctrine. The more you can show you are at one with the doctrine, repeating the doctrine to your teams and counterparts, thus taking it very seriously, the better your chances of climbing up through the ranks. Better still if you spend time with other workmates that reinforce the doctrine and mantra of company culture.

Groupthink

'Groupthink is a psychological phenomenon that occurs within a group of people in which the desire for harmony or conformity in the group results in an irrational or dysfunctional decision-making outcome. Cohesiveness, or the desire for cohesiveness, in a group may produce a tendency among its members to agree at all costs.' (Ref Wikipedia)

Groupthink's most destructive impact is when pushing to form a consensus. People aim for a consensus, thinking (mistakenly) that backing the group idea gives the idea strength rather than working logically through the pros and cons of the alternatives which may be more suited to addressing the actual need.

The desire to conform wholly with the policies handed down from the senior team and openly enforcing these policies whilst rewarding 'proper' behaviour with further inclusion and acceptance into the group is a divisive tool that can be at play in organisations right up to boardroom level. A direct negative consequence of groupthink is debunking an individual's objectivity and critical thinking when it is seen to be at odds with the beliefs of the group, e.g. in *Lord of the Flies*, groupthink affected the boys' reasoning and their resulting actions which defied their individual sense of judgment and morality.

'The end justifies the means' is another negative consequence of groupthink, where you justify behaviour that on a personal level you are just not comfortable with but on an organisational level you buy into for the 'greater good'.

Shunning

Those who do not stay in step with group policies are routinely shunned and/or expelled.

Senior organisation members are the most vulnerable to shunning, in particular those who choose to become clones or groupies of the group leader so as to further espouse their loyalty, helping them to climb the greasy pole. In being seen to be in tune with senior management groupthink, some take it upon themselves to call out those that think differently, effectively shunning them from the group.

Tips for leaving the cult of the organisation

Just like helping someone exit a cult, anyone leaving the corporate field after a significant period needs to be given time to re-calibrate themselves, their family and their natural living environment. Given that significant life energy has been spent ensconced with the organisation's needs and beliefs, this freeing oneself of the organisation's thought and control structures can take time and will hit many peaks and troughs. You may feel sometimes as though you are at war with yourself and you may not be aware of just how deeply ingrained some of the belief systems can be within your own subconscious, especially if you have been with the organisation a number of years.

From my own experience, I would advise:

- Re-establishing healthy relationships with yourself and your family in a gentle, open way, at your own pace
- Empowering yourself to think critically and openly assessing the pros and cons of your experience will also help you evaluate and steer your own journey forward
- Acting without judgment, forgiving and accepting yourself right now and, when necessary, cocooning yourself as you work through the emotional roller-coaster

The aim here is to restore your creative, authentic self, minus the groupthink you may have been routinely exposed to for a very long time, thereby freeing up any inner blockages or thought control and enabling yourself to be the full, bright and beautiful soul you were born to be.

Reflection

Some corporations can choose to develop a cult-like work culture to enable employees to become successfully entrained with the organisation's ideology.

Tasks

Reviewing the cult-like tendencies outlined in this chapter, which of these may be at play in your own organisation? What steps can you take to protect your own ingenuity, credibility and critical thinking capability?

CHAPTER 11

How Corporates Function

In this chapter, I describe the formation of corporations and how they work, as well as looking at some work studies that enable us to stand back from our part in the piece to see the drivers at play.

A corporation is an organisation – usually a group of people or a company – authorised by the state to act as a single entity (a legal entity recognised by private and public law 'born out of statute'; a legal person in legal context) and recognised as such in law for certain purposes.

https://en.wikipedia.org/wiki/Corporation#:~:text=The%20concept%20of%20the%20corporation%20was,body%20politic%20to%20describe%20the%20state.&text=The%20concept%20of%20the,to%20describe%20the%20state.&text=of%20the%20corporation%20was,body%20politic%20to%20describe

The words 'corporate' and 'corpse' are actually derived from the same Latin root word, 'corpus', meaning body.

When you *incorporate* a company, a transformation akin to that of the creator Victor Frankenstein and his unsuspecting monster occurs. Incorporating a company essentially turns it into a person that is considered human in the eyes of the law. Like us humans, corporations have to adhere to the law and pay taxes, yet when a corporation fails, *unlike us,* its shareholder, managers and employees are *not* responsible for its debts – this is known as limited liability. The ultimate aim of the 'incorporation' is to exist beyond the lives of its creators who will ultimately die. Corporates are even developed to have personalities (they are developed through their cultures that leak into our broader world – think of the verb 'Google' and how we use that each and every day).

'Corporation'. *Vocabulary.com Dictionary,* Vocabulary.com https://www.vocabulary.com/dictionary/corporation. Accessed 14 July 2023

Stewart Kyd authored the first treatise on corporate law, stating that a corporation is *'a collection of many individuals united into one body, under a special denomination, having perpetual succession under an artificial form, and vested, by the policy of the law, with the capacity of acting, in several respects, as an individual, particularly of taking and granting property, of contracting obligations, and of suing and being sued, of enjoying privileges and immunities in common, and of exercising a variety of political rights, more or less extensive, according to the design of its institution, or the powers conferred upon it, either at the time of its creation or at any subsequent period of its existence.'*

A Treatise on the Law of Corporations, Stewart Kyd (1793–1794)

Today, we understand a corporate as a body of people who work together to achieve a particular set of unified goals, whether that is returning X amount of profit each year to their shareholders, expanding their global reach, or reducing their workforce with the uptake of AI, etc. All corporates have agreed goals that the corporate body will work towards each year. Whether you are aware of what the overarching organisational goals are or not, each sub-division of the corporate will have a subset of goals that ultimately link back to the mothership's game plan to ensure that each resource is deployed and expended to an optimum level to meet the organisation's targets and, to the definition above, continue to do so long into the future after the initial founders have passed, thus immortalising our Frankenstein monster.

Broadening the scope of the corporate structure, we find multi-national corporations which have a global reach; these may also be referred to as a multi-national or transnational enterprises. These entities typically own and oversee the provision or production of goods and services in more than one country.

https://en.wikipedia.org/wiki/Multinational_corporation, Accessed 10 August 2023

How do corporates work?

Corporates are mostly built using a hierarchical topology, ensuring a chain of command from top to bottom, just like in military endeavours; this enables efficient decision-making and messaging, and management of people across the organisation. At the top of the corporate tree, you will find the C-suite executives working within this range of roles:

- Chief accounting officer (CAO)
- Chief executive officer (CEO)
- Chief financial officer (CFO)

- Chief marketing officer (CMO)
- Chief information security officer (CISO)
- Chief procurement officer (CPO)
- Chief sustainability officer (CSO)
- Chief technology officer (CTO)
- Chief operating officer (COO)
- Chief information officer (CIO)

Beneath this layer you have middle management who are responsible for ensuring the work gets done the right way across an array of departments including HR, Marketing, Sales, IT & Finance. Below this are the front-line staff.

A company's chain of command depends on whether it is vertical or horizontally structured. A vertical company's chain of command typically runs from the CEO at the top, delegating down through a number of hierarchical tiers to lower-level managers, down to junior team members. A horizontal company's chain of command (typically smaller businesses with less employees) is usually less hierarchical as it relies on a flatter structure, giving managers more responsibilities.

The chain of command is essential for efficient running of the organisation by:

- Eliminating confusion
- Providing clear lines of accountability
- Improving the ease of decision making

However, it can have its downsides:

- Lack of agility especially if the organisation is very hierarchical

- Slow communication and less collaboration, especially if there are too many decision-makers in the process
- Employees don't feel as empowered in this type of structure with so many decision-makers

Separate and completely independent to the company's management team mentioned above, every corporate has a board of directors. The structure and powers of the board are detailed in the initial articles of incorporation and the corporate bylaws (these can determine the number of board members, how board members are elected, and when the board meets on a regular basis). It is the role of the board to make decisions on behalf of the company and its shareholders, by guiding how the interests of the shareholders are protected, how the company is protected against risk, how stakeholders are communicated with, etc. The overall aim is to ensure the company is run as effectively as possible whilst being in adherence with the laws of the country in which it operates.

It is important to note that the real control of the company lies with the shareholders, so it is necessary that both the CEO and the company's board drive an agenda that ultimately protects the shareholders' interests, eg. their dividends, growing their profit, etc, though these investors and institutions often remain invisible. It is feasible, though, for corporate executives like the CEO to hold substantial share positions in order to control voting rights.

So, in summary, corporates are legal entities that have a board of directors who are responsible for setting the overarching company agenda that will deliver the shareholders' profit and strategic benefits, with the C-Suite management team responsible for overseeing the company activities that will meet this agenda and, lastly, the workers executing the tasks that ensure the company's targets are met. A small handful of core shareholders receive the profit of global worker labour and in turn this money can drive individual world economies to varying degrees.

There are two distinct groups of shareholding:

1) Diffuse shareholding by external investors who themselves pick the board that will monitor the company management team

2) Concentrated block-holding by insiders who monitor the work of the management team directly

A block-holder (this can be either an individual or an organisation) owns a large block of a company's shares (usually 5% or more). Block-holders are often able to influence the company with voting rights associated with their holdings, ultimately the more shares they own, the stronger the influence on the decision-making of the company and its overall agenda and ambition.

www.Investopedia.com Accessed: 07-08-2023

As well as understanding the mechanics of the board, it is important, I feel, to understand who the corporate owners are, especially if a corporate entity has very politically motivated owners who may well be directing the course of business for some of the world's highest revenue earning companies that in turn employ significant numbers of people like you and I to carry out the related 'work'.

Corporate wealth

The people who own the top global revenue generating companies and how they perform their role as shareholders is bound to be of economy-wide importance due to the financial flow as well as the millions of workers employed. Here is a bird's eye view of some of the world's largest revenue generating companies:

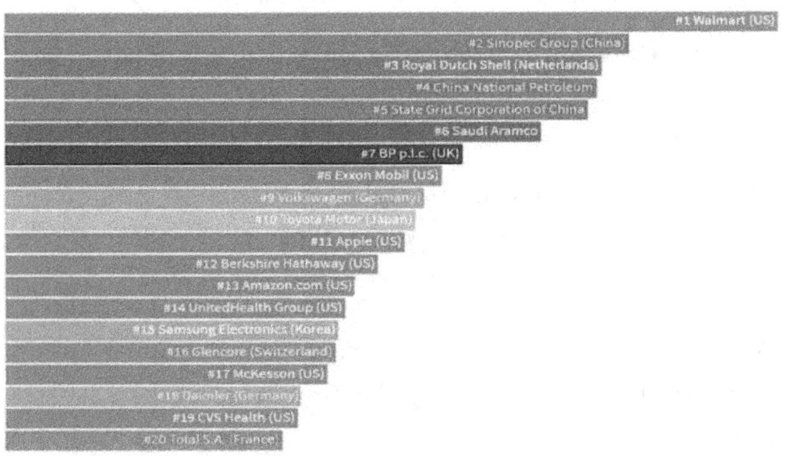

www.theenumeration.com/largest-companies-in-the-world/
Accessed 8 August 2023

Below is a summary view of the industries generating the highest revenues and the number of global employees they employ and, in turn, whose profits turn the wheels of our world economy:

Industry	Sum of Employees	Profit in USD Millions
Financial Services	2,546,907	**$286,748.7**

Oil and gas	2,073,628	**$215,433.7**
Electronics	1,247,281	**$133,961.8**
Automotive	1,489,412	**$87,547.9**
Information technology	337,500	**$137,304**
Retail	5,329,957	**$70,467.2**
Healthcare	932,990	**$39,928.2**
Telecommunications	202,600	**$20,081**
Conglomerate	80,728	**$8,345.8**
Commodities	90,315	**$8,074**
Construction	1,045,977	**$8,000.8**
Electricity	871,145	**$7,137.8**
Insurance	182,646	**$3,087.1**
Steel	230,884	**$2,994.9**
Chemicals	220,760	**−$197.7**

CHAPTER 12

Corporate Engagement

Next, let us consider the level of engagement from corporate workers across the globe. Reviewing the latest Gallup *'State of the Workplace report'*, one starts to see how a blend of cultural, economic and ideological factors shape the level of a global worker's corporate engagement. From reviewing the charts in the report, I wondered if perhaps those countries with higher corporate engagement such as India and the Americas display a higher level of corporate buy-in possibly necessitated by economic need and cultural groupthink compared with the lowest level of corporate work engagement in Europe. Could this be because Europeans are less likely to buy into corporate ideology? Naturally, lower engagement will follow in jurisdictions that have access to less global corporates overall (Africa and China, for example). There are many reasons why we see such varying levels of engagement as we move across our globe.

https://www.gallup.com/workplace/349484/state-of-the-global-workplace-2022-report.aspx Accessed 10 July 2022

Whilst employees may not be *physically* leaving corporates, they may instead be 'quiet-quitting'.

'Quiet quitting describes the situation when an employee mentally and

emotionally checks out from their job, and does the bare minimum to get by.'

https://dictionary.cambridge.org/dictionary/english/queit-quitting Accessed 12 July 2023

Quiet quitting is so prevalent across the corporate sphere that even at the 2023 World Economic Forum's Annual Meeting in Davos a session on 'Quiet quitting and the Meaning of Work' was held with a panel of industry leaders who outlined four key ways to create a company culture that will engage and retain talent to try and address the quiet quitting phenomena and give work more meaning:

1. Learn how to nurture your talent

2. Offer a sense of purpose

3. Personalise the digital experience

4. Hold entry and exit interviews

Undoubtedly work stress has a key part to play with people opting to leave or disengage from the workforce – see the Gallup *State of the Workplace* report's stress chart for more illuminating details.

https://www.gallup.com/workplace/349484/state-of-the-global-workplace.aspx Accessed 12 July 2023

To get an idea of how many people we are talking about in terms of the global workforce, according to ILO, the International Labour Organisation, there are approximately 65,000 multi-nationals employing around 90 million people globally.

https://www.ilo.org/global/publications/world-of-work-magazine/articles/WCMS_091639/lang--en/index.htm
Accessed 15 July 2023

In 2021, talk of the Great Resignation across all walks of media saw the national active quit-rate double, with almost 50 million Americans quitting their jobs that year. Today, it looks like this attrition phase is coming to a close, possibly due to the subsequent rise in inflation/interest rates, with workers more likely to try to hold on to their jobs, however, this will not prevent companies looking to protect their bottom line and look for further efficiencies to improve it, which ultimately results in layoffs.

In *The Importance of Work in an Age of Uncertainty*[2], author David Blustein, a Boston professor, suggests that in the last few decades alone workers are losing an increasing level of protection and autonomy and, worse still, are being increasingly treated like commodities.

Work stress can also arise from the type of work we do, particularly if we are employed by someone else in exchange for our livelihood. Essentially work can be broken down into jobs that either contribute to the betterment of the world in which we live or those that do not, i.e. those that are harder to illicit any true meaning from if you are looking at the bigger picture and looking to understand the worth of what you do in our broader society.

https://doi.org/10.1093/oso/9780190213701.001.0001

---

[2] Blustein, D. L (2019) *The Importance of work in an age of uncertainty: The eroding work experience in America.* Oxford University Press.

Bullshit Jobs: A Theory by anthropologist David Graeber *'postulates the existence of meaningless jobs and analyzes their societal harm. He contends that over half of societal work is pointless and becomes psychologically destructive when paired with a work ethic that associates work with self-worth … a form of paid employment that is so completely pointless, unnecessary, or pernicious that even the employee cannot justify its existence … largely in the private sector. They {the worker} believe that work determines their self-worth, even as they find that work pointless. Graeber describes this cycle as 'a scar across our collective soul'… populations occupied with busy work have less time to revolt.'*

Graeber breaks down bullshit jobs into five groups:

1. Flunkies who are seen to have no value within the organisation, 'who serve to make their superiors feel important'
2. Goons who have value in the organisation, but not to society in general
3. Duct tapers who 'temporarily fix problems that could be fixed permanently'
4. Box tickers, who 'create the appearance that something useful is being done when it is not'
5. Taskmasters, the enforcers if you like 'who create extra work for those who do not need it[3]

https://en.m.wikipedia.org/wiki/Bullshit_Jobs Accessed 10 September 2023

If I had to consider which group my last job fell into, it would be that of the goon, where I was seen to have value in the organisation but when you stripped it back and looked at

---

[3] Copyright 2018 by David Graeber. All rights reserved. Reprinted by permission of the David Graeber Estate: https://davidgraeber.org

it from the outside in, the reality on pulling the curtains back was not so pretty. The ugly truth is that I contributed absolutely nothing to society (apart from hiring and mentoring some really wonderfully talented people) and this, in fact, was the burning heart of the reason behind my final corporate disengagement. When I weighed up the social impact of my role, I could only think of it as making the wealthy wealthier and achieving nothing much else besides. Businesses are routinely put under pressure to stream-line business processing, oftentimes requiring a reduction in FTE (Full Time Employee) aka letting people go, amongst other optimization measures. It can be difficult to square-off the goal of saving a ludicrously wealth-laden corporate more money, just so the share price is protected. In corporate-land, hallowed financial saves are often seen as the big win and achieving this can surely help you get promoted quicker:

Optimized business processing + cutting headcount can equal corporate success.

When I stopped to consider what my job really meant in terms of social value, i.e. where was the social advantage and how was the betterment of society to be achieved through my industrious achievements, it just did not exist and, even worse, I could see all the risks associated with the latest industry advances, aka 'transformation' programs that loom large in every organisation these days due to pressure from shareholders and clients to get access to the latest and greatest ways of doing things, as quickly as possible. The conflicting factors at play weighed heavily on me, despite the industry reassurances that this is the way of things, this is how you become a leader in your field, you do whatever you have to do at all costs to meet your goals and to receive that corporate adulation.

I cannot help thinking that we have choices here to slow things down, for companies to be more prudent in their need to transform and expand but instead the demands of the world economy determine that everyone, including employees, business processing, support and technology should be 'always on', data should be 'always available' and with it continuous dedicated support to handle things when they go wrong because things *always* go wrong – that is one unassailable truth I have learnt throughout my career; it's how you choose to orchestrate and treat people that matters.

I also decided that I fundamentally did not want to be part of any industry that enabled the smooth and pernicious investment or support of fossil fuels. How could I look at myself or my children squarely in the face and say, 'I am doing a good job', when inwardly I considered how I was doing my bit to kill the planet? Not intentionally, of course, but I certainly was part of the problem and that was a truth I could no longer contain or carry. You can get behind all the charity events you like but in the end, if the industry you are a part of is doing something that damages others or the environment, then you have to question your role in that. Even if you are just passively working in it, putting your very life energy into enabling that construct to achieve those goals has to be challenged.

So, in questioning my part in all that, something had to give and it seemed clear to me in the haze of it all, when the pieces of my life felt like they were falling asunder, that I had one significant life choice to make. I could choose what seemed like the easy option, i.e. to continue on as I was – to wallow in the rut I had created for myself and my family, which eventually would in time make me chronically ill given the level of dis-ease I was feeling with my working life to-date, all in exchange for the comfortable, material world my family thought they safely inhabited. Alternatively, I could make what seemed a rationally holistic and life-affirming decision that would entail walking away from a corporate career that just felt like b*****t if I am to be completely honest. It was a job that I was always embarrassed to share the detail on when strangers asked me what I did for a living and why I chose to do it. Yes, I could lead with the schmooze, sharing snippets of genius of being able to change X into Y, but it was hardly water into wine, and the shady reality was that I chose to do it not only for the money but also to stroke my own ego, that I had reached such a position from humble working-class beginnings as a worker in an industry that seemed to become more toxic the higher you climbed. I had allowed myself to fully buy into the delusion that I was really achieving something here.

So, my one and only soul-preserving course of action that would assert my own brand of ethics and life values (as opposed to a set of corporate values which I become practically brainwashed into believing were my own), as well as showing my kids that, yes, you can alter your course in life and more importantly you can choose to take steps to do good, was easy really in the end; you just get up and walk away (of course, the children may not have liked the outcome when it directly affected them – see Chapter 9 on Family Impact!).

Reflection

We are more stressed than we have ever been, having less time and more money but things inevitably costing more, meaning most of us may have less materially than our parents had, with a lot of families struggling to ever get a first home let alone all the security that is supposed to go with a mortgage (a life-long loan) – so where does this leave us and what can we do about it?

Taking a step back (see Chapter 5 as a start) and really reviewing what we feel will make us deeply happy, rather than just going along with the status quo so we can be materially happy, is an important checkpoint for every worker.

If your overarching life goal is to have all the material things you feel you need to survive, or that perhaps your parents never had, and you are willing to sign up to that for the rest of your life to get it, then you're all set.

However, if you feel you would like to understand more about what would make you truly happy and have an opportunity to do something about it, then just do it – why wait?

We humans surely must be meant to be more than just workers in the corporate factories of today (set to become tomorrow's AI fodder). Don't we at least deserve a moment in our lives to find out what our true self wants for the betterment of ourselves, our families and the society within which we exist?

We do have choices, albeit difficult ones involving money and how we choose to live, what we choose to think about and the level of joy we can expect as part of our life journey. It all ultimately comes down to *expectation* and what we are willing to exchange to meet those life expectations, at the very least just being aware of the trade-off given we have been granted the gift of an organic, free-flowing life; we should at every opportunity exercise that freedom.

Consider, if you will, people that do not have *any* choice due to living under fascist rule, refugee camps, imprisonment, etc — what they would give to have the right to choose a life of their own making! If you are reading this book, you are one of the luckier ones: you already have demonstrated a choice in choosing what you read and what you do with that knowledge.

Task

If you have any takeaways or light-bulb moments after reading this section, record them now along with any meaningful actions you wish to take.

CHAPTER 13

Corporate Burnout and Boreout

There is constant speculation on the impact of corporate burnout and why it is continuing to grow and what we need to do about it. First, though – what is it?

Burnout, according to the Cambridge dictionary, is *'the state of having no energy or enthusiasm because of working too hard, or someone who shows the effects of this state'*.

https://dictionary.cambridge.org/dictionary/english/burnout Accessed 20 September 2023

Dr. Ben Wigert (Gallup's director of research and strategy for Workplace Management) held a podcast discussion on employee burnout in August 2023, where it was suggested that a significant number of employees in the US are experiencing the effects of burnout. See here for more details:

https://www.gallup.com/workplace/508898/employee-burnout-causes-cures/aspx Access 20 September 2023

So, it appears that manager burnout in particular is getting worse; could this be primarily due to disengagement or disenchantment with the corporate workplace?

This is not just an American phenomenon; it is most certainly a global issue, given most of the big corporates now operate at a global level with a global workforce. In fact, it's a problem that is snowballing its way across the globe when you stop and think about it and that makes for a lot of unhappy people!

Do I think burnout was at play in my physical breakdown leading to my own corp*exit*? Absolutely! The mask of physical illness was only symptomatic of routine bouts of mental and physical exhaustion that came and went over the years when my system became overloaded from the build-up of toxic work stress and worries. We may be aware that these stresses are lying latent in our bodies, carried around with us each and every day, and yes, we can take personal steps to try to improve our well-being through a variety of means such as:

- yoga or meditation

- the gym

- taking a wellness day or sabbatical work when really needed

- counselling to target the issues (often offered free through your corporate medical insurance)

- reorganising your workload, and perhaps your family's workload, by redistributing responsibility

However, what is often much harder to address is a potentially toxic corporate culture in your place of employment that has its own agenda and which is beyond your control to 'fix'. Absolutely you can discuss with your manager the options for achieving a more sustainable work-life balance, but often there is no panacea, with corporates increasingly looking to get people to be more productive to ensure protection of that company bottom line.

So, what specifically is causing the burnout? I decided to check with the experts and in doing so discovered a book that goes to the heart of the matter.

*The Burnout Epidemic: The Rise of Chronic Stress and How we can fix it** is a book written by Jennifer Moss explaining the underlying causes of burnout and why it is work culture rather than the individual that needs to change to address it, a worthy guide of our time that resonated with my own very real burnout experience.

What is Boreout?

Boredom at work or 'boreout' is considered to be just as harmful as burnout. Boreout is caused where you become so chronically bored with the work you are doing to the point you think it is meaningless or devoid of any real value. This can happen as a result of working like a factory hen where the environment you work in is rigid and unstimulating or when you feel under-challenged in what you do or you feel constantly overlooked, leaving you with a lack of motivation or interest. This sounds on the surface like an unimportant and almost nice-to-have phenomena until you consider that boreout can lead to the exact same set of chronic illnesses identified for burnout, i.e. depression, anxiety and varying degrees of physical symptoms depending on the level of dis-ease the worker has with their work life.

So, some thought on not just improving the physical environment (see my chapter on the Future of Work — Changing the Working Environment) but engaging workers so they are energised in what they do can prevent worker turnover or, worse, continued ambivalence. Aligning workers with collaboration opportunities (talking to others can be a great way to see different viewpoints) and helping workers identify their unique skills or how to become proficient in something they would like to be good at through the use of mentoring or coaching can help move workers out of a boreout rut.[4]

Reflection

So, the next time you are checking in with yourself, have a think about how the organisation you work for may be contributing to your overall stress. Identifying what you can do to help yourself is a good step to get to a state of optimal health but also gives clarity on which of the reasons above may be driving you to a state of burnout. Understanding where you can do something to help yourself versus being at the mercy of unhealthy corporate practices is essential to help you make the best decision for your working life. It may also be useful to discuss any corporate-related concerns with your colleagues to both validate your own observations and support each other in identifying active ways in which to address it – or not, as the case might be.

Tasks

What stresses are apparent within your workplace and what

---

[4] Moss, J (2021) *The Burnout Epidemic: The Rise of Chronic Stress and How we can fix it.* Harvard Business Review Press.

steps, if any, can you take to address them? For example, discuss with HR, your boss, your colleagues, launch an initiative to bring visibility to it. What personal action can you take to aid your own well-being?

CHAPTER 14

The Corp*exit* Survey Results

To understand how my experience of leaving the corporate world compared with those from the broader public, I first decided to run a simple survey, the results of which prove to be fairly consistent across the board. Here are the questions and responses:

Question 1: What would be your reason for leaving your corporate job?

This open question received a myriad responses which all coalesce around a series of themes; I have shared a handful here:

- Politics: "Tired of office politics", "Politics drives a negative agenda", "Negative management due to politics …"

- Bad culture: "Cheesy corporate culture", "Surveillance and monitoring made me question the culture", "Fake culture … a pool table and free snacks do not represent a good working culture."

- Presenteeism: "Company wants you to practically live on site despite emphasising that they offer a good work-life balance", "Need to be seen both online and in the office from dawn till dusk", "Being seen on site is the only way to progress in the organisation."

- Poor management: "Management are up their own ass", "Poor leadership who focus on managing up rather than connecting with the workforce", "Inexperienced people managers who either are afraid or just clueless on how to back their team …"

Question 2: After leaving your corporate job, how did you feel?

The responses from the multiple choices offered were unanimous:

i.   Elated – 100% of answers

ii. Terrified at what the future might hold

iii. I felt mainly positive about my next step

iv. I wish I had stayed where I was

v.   All the above

vi. Other

Question 3: What do you wish you had known or done before making the transition?

This open question has some fairly common themes:

- Money: "Saved money", "Sorted my finances", "Stopped spending", "Ceased my credit card", "Paid off loans"

- Communication: "Prepped my family", "Told the company how I really felt", "Discussed in depth with my partner", "Got my team ready"

- Support: "Got guidance on how to proceed; I felt helpless", "Hired a therapist!", "Talked about it with my friends", "Working with a career coach would have proved useful."

Question 4: What has improved in your life as a result of your decision?

Again, this is an open question with consistent responses:

- Family relations: "Quality of my time spent with people I love", "I no longer snap at my family members", "I can be spontaneous and have fun again", "I am a nicer person, or so they tell me."

- Time: "Time to do the things I love", "I have time to breathe", "I don't begrudge sharing my time with others", "I live every day!", "I relish getting up early in the morning now, to spend my time on the things that matter to me."

- Well-being: "Happier all round", "I feel like a whole person", "I sleep at night", "I can breathe properly", "I have less anxiety", "I feel more connected with the world around me", "I no longer feel angry."

Question 5: Have there been any negative consequences in your life since?

There was one overall resounding response to this: "No!", as well as: "Stressed at having no income", "I feel I have lost the structure in my day", "I miss my work colleagues who had become friends."

Question 6: What have you transitioned to doing since?

i. A public sector role: 8%

ii. Working for a not-for-profit: 9%

iii. Setting up my own business: 35%

iv. Working as a contractor/freelancer: 38%

v. Retirement: 6%

vi. Voluntary work or caring for a relative: 3%

vii. Nothing I am unemployed: 2%

viii. Other (please specify)

Question 7: Do you have any regrets?

The overwhelming response to this question was "No".

Question 8: What would you say to anyone thinking of doing the same?

The responses to this question were positive and clear:

"Just do it", "Do it today!", "Go ahead", "It will be alright", "Don't wait another day", "Carpe diem"

Question 9: How do you look at corporate life now? List anything corporates get wrong or can improve on.

This open question received mixed responses:

"A waste of my time; I wish I had known this earlier."

"I feel sorry for people who are stuck on the corporate treadmill. If they put people rather than their own investors first, things might be different."

"The ends justify the means, or so they would have you believe"

"It is slavery, pure and simple."

"Red tape and company culture suck."

"They are energy sapping cowboys."

"Boring, dull place to work …"

"Greasy poles with greasy management leave oil all over you."

"I wouldn't go back if you paid me, though the money would come in useful right now."

"I am master of my own destiny now rather than the unhappy brainwashed robot my family had to put up with for years."

"It's a total misuse of your talents! Corporates fail to really listen to people; they are so caught up generating their own spin on culture … they love the sound of their own voice."

Question 10: If you had to make the decision again, would you?

i. I would do it again: 21%

ii. I would delay the decision: 12%

iii. I would have done it earlier: 67%

iv. No I would not do it again: 0%

CHAPTER 15

Planning for the Future

Taking the next step

My career coach telling me 'Your next step is just that – it is just your next step' allowed me to take a tentative step forward without having to have it all worked out. When I would be thinking forward and pressing myself to figure out what the future might hold, I found myself getting caught up in a worry-wall of stress around making the 'right' next move. It became a sweat zone of intent, like a tightrope walker that cannot afford to put one step wrong; this is how I felt about moving forward. Having gained my freedom, I was conscious of squandering any opportunity and I did not want to commit the same mistake again. I paralyzed myself with all my good intention – I was literally afraid to put a foot wrong.

So, how was I going to get the next step right? The ego pressed me day and night: *'How are you going to get yourself out of this one and put back everything you tore apart?'* Suddenly, I couldn't make any decision, not even the tiniest one (enter the tool of acceptance). Aware that I had to put something on my LinkedIn to show I had actually left the building of my corporate job, I agonised over how I might present things so

I could show the world that, yes, I had made a change and in fact I was now moving on. I settled on putting a placeholder on LinkedIn which allowed me to clearly show I had finished my last role (I chose not to advertise it but let people come across it if they were looking for an update). I was looking to place-hold with something neutral that would buy me time until I could actually work out what my next move should be. So, I settled on 'working freelance'. Once my status was in place, it felt like I could hit pause and take time to reflect, instead of simply reacting to work requests.

Hitting pause gave the ultimate relief as if all that pent-up desire and frustration could just be let go and I could step out of the cage of my own making into the light, blink a while at the sunshine and start to enjoy the limitless abundance that now seemed to offer itself to me, little by little each day. Drawing this line under my last corporate episode was what allowed me paradoxically to move forward. I could have written anything, really, e.g. volunteering, interning, education; so many more paths unfolding and available but now whilst being on pause I was no longer in a rush to stick a label on it … Freelance consultancy suited me fine until I figured out the rest and I did not honestly know how long that might be. In work I had been a quick-fire responder, always solutioning and resolving on the spot, working through tasks at high speed, but here I owed myself something more than just 'completing the task'; if anything I needed to stop thinking in this robotic, reactive manner. I owed myself more than just a 'get the task completed approach' when it came to triaging my life. All life-related decisions would by their nature be messier and have more impact, so I had to find another way to do a life/career triage.

To help me untangle, I decided I really needed to enlist the help of a life coach, and my goodness, how the universe weaved its magic! The 'flow' delivered literally within 24 hours! I had an unsolicited call from a coach I had worked with previously, offering me three free hours – this opportunity gave me quite the rush as it signalled to me that the universal flow was indeed back in my life, without me having to control or manipulate an outcome. My heartfelt desire manifested what I needed, exactly when I needed it. It felt like a greenlight had been granted, reassuring me that somehow I really was on the right path after all.

From this moment, I promised myself that I would look broader, deeper, brighter instead of the constricted rung of steps I had steered myself to follow for fear of slipping off the high-wire. I felt strongly that there was no need to ricochet into a similar role; instead, my coach advised me to step back and really figure out what I actually liked doing versus what I could live with, to work out what I wanted to offer the world. In tandem with this, I was also figuring out my financial minimum; how much I actually needed to float the home-ship so I could start to identify the broadest set of opportunities albeit within my own set of constraints.

It was at this point that I pulled together a simple life skills list (see Appendix B). This was a way of bringing together what I loved doing and prioritising those lesser skills to help determine where to best focus my energy. I pulled together a simple list of core values that underpin the desires and actions in my life – mine being Freedom, Inspiration, Innovation and Grace. All of this brought into focus the *types of activity* that would *align* with those very *core values*. At last I felt we were getting somewhere and, remembering my coach's sage advice that my next job was just my next job – no more, no less – massively took the pressure out of it and, dare I say it, brought back the fun.

I had to figure out how much money I felt I needed to make in order to do the things I needed, how often I wanted to work and in what way I would take this action – would I want to sit at home all day, working remotely from a laptop? Would I want to be locked away on a work-site where I would continue to fight through rush-hour traffic? Or would I like to feel a sense of flexibility around my 'doing' that allowed me to do as I fancied but on my own terms – this was a no-brainer. I knew I did not want to go back to the five-day week slog – it was way too demanding; too much time taken for one activity leaving so little for the rest of my life, myself, my family, my friends, volunteering. This needed time too, and I wanted balance, a lot more balance than a five-day week would ever be able to give me. The problem was that all full-time jobs demanded this level of commitment, and a four-day week is almost impossible to achieve unless you start on the five-day then wait patiently to see if they will allow a four-day week, and if they don't, you are essentially back to square one. You can of course ask at the interview stage but it's highly likely you will be disregarded as a result. You could of course arrive at a four-and-a-half-day week possibly, but this is not guaranteed and agencies are quick to let you know that new employers are just not open to anything less than a five-day week for full-time roles.

So, I decided I would focus on contract work and contour my time with the agencies as three days per week maximum. Since they would only be paying me by the day, it worked for some companies, too. Contract work also has the benefit of no longer having to carry all that crushing responsibility that is part and parcel of a senior position which involves managing a team, global stakeholders, budgets and keeping to the party line. No, the contract would release me from all of those demands and allow me to focus purely on the doing. I realised that the manna of the ego is the *doing*; how she purred, though now I had contained her, squarely bounded by my real needs, and this time she would no longer be allowed to drive me towards any insane working hours, schedule or commitments. No – she was a shadow of her former dictatorial self now, contained by the forces that needed to do other things with my time. The soul shone brightly now, given the soul-saving oxygen that was being released; it was invigorating my depths, everything seemed to have more colour, more taste, more vibrancy, as if I was well and truly alive, so I knew I was on the right path. The flow had returned – that languid easiness in your life that lets you know you are now barrelling along the soul's highway once more. The ego knew her game was up, she could no longer shout so loud or reach the controls, we were driving towards an unknown but far more thrilling destination than I could have imagined, no more clawing my way up a corporate ladder at the expense of myself and those in my life, not for me … not for anyone! This was *my* gig now and no one was going to steer my ship but me and that felt good.

CHAPTER 16

Ditch the Toxic Corporate Quirks

As part of surviving in my corporate existence as long as I did, I have unconsciously over the years developed some quirks that I identify now as potentially life-toxic and which needed to be shed to enable me to move into the next period of my life unfettered. These, in no particular order, are as follows:

- The need to be 'always on' and in control as I rise at the crack of dawn each day, starting earlier than everyone else to get a head-start so I am either on top of or ready to tackle the curve-balls in the day ahead. On the face of it, this sounds like a great trait to foster, i.e. to be prepared ahead of schedule, however, doing this on a routine basis not only ends up with you losing valuable sleep or family time, it also can stymie your ability to work on the spot; just jump in and deal with things rather than taking an hour or two ahead of the race to feel on top of things. Letting go of the control stick has really allowed me to firstly breathe better as I am no longer trying to hold onto everything ridiculously tightly in case it spins out of control; secondly, it has allowed spontaneity and a lightness to enter my life as I create room in my world for more of the unknown which does not have to be seen as threatening, rather it allows opportunities for growth and learning to take place.

- The need to follow up incessantly until the job is done, which may seem like a positive seeing as you are actively keeping on top of things until they are completed, however, not only does it keep you worrying subconsciously about something getting done, it also stops you from really delegating properly and thus empowering people to do what they do best. It has to be better to leave it up to the person you have assigned it to, to provide you with updates whilst they are doing it, putting the onus on *them* rather than you; this now includes assignments to family members!

- Worrying about people and their work-life balance – this was something I carried as a manager, always wanting to ensure my team were properly cared for but, like the last point, might it not be better to let them look after their own work-life balance and come to you only if there is something they need your help with, thus treating them like the professionals they are rather than you would a family member?

- The need to be seen – if you are working as an individual contributor or managing a relatively small team within a large corporate, it can feel as though you need to take every opportunity to be 'visible', so the broader group can see the achievements; this becomes exhausting, even seeing those same faces over and over who are trying to achieve the same so they can win that promotion, that funding, the accolades in the organization ... it becomes a race. Might a better approach be to create a weekly or monthly bulletin that summarises the team's key achievements and send it out to the pertinent group you are looking to gain attention from, thus taking back some of your time and cataloguing your achievements to boot?

- The need to win every point – failure can become a pressure-point depending on the way it is dealt with in an organisation. Without failure, though, some of the most important innovations may not have been honed to reach their maximum potential. Letting go of the attachment to success by clearly stating the success criteria, as well as learning from the project (in particular where failures have helped improve the project outcomes), enables you to not put such pressure on winning every time. Acknowledging the journey and what it taught you along the way is what counts.

- The need to be liked – it is virtually impossible to control the reaction of anyone to your way of doing things; some will be positive about your approach and others either neutral or even negative. Dispensing with your attachment to how people regard you will free you up no end. Obviously, read the room, but my point is to not take it personally or carry it with you. Acknowledge any constructive criticism and disregard the rest. We are all learning all of the time.

Reflection

The art of survival and being successful in corporate life can imbue us with some toxic quirks that it would do us well to shed before entering the next fresh-faced chapter.

Tasks

What toxic quirks do you feel it would serve you well to stop so that you can enter your next chapter without shame or judgment, to ensure you are a blank canvas, open to all possibilities?

CHAPTER 17

Life a year on

This chapter focuses on what I am doing today versus this time last year, and what perspectives have changed during that time.

So, a year on, is my life utterly transformed? Not quite; like a journey you take with the kids when they incessantly ask 'are we nearly there yet?', my reply is, 'we'll be there soon I'm sure, for now just enjoy the journey.' Life is certainly feeling a lot more relaxed, fun and colourful, though (see my next chapter to get a close-up on the material benefits experienced since exiting).

A year ago, I felt like I was focusing a significant portion of my life energy on progressing a corporate career up the steep and thorny ladder to gain more accolades, more stripes for my corporate uniform and, as I have shared inwardly, I was not at ease with where I was going or how I was spending my time and what it all ultimately meant in the greater scheme of things. One year on, my perspectives have completely shifted, both as a result of life bringing me experiences that may have come one way or another, the difference being that I had a different head-space to face them.

The first major experience came in the form of my father

receiving a significant cancer diagnosis. If I think of how I would have handled this along with my corporate career, I would have made it a priority to help and support where I could but probably in the grand scheme of corporate life I would have had fairly significant timetabling and commitments to work around to release time and energy to physically be there for my parents. As I now had the life-space to make him my number one priority, it meant I could actively help by taking him for treatment, cooking for him and eventually acting as carer after he had a particularly bad fall. I consider this time with both my parents a privilege, to be honest; somehow I had been gifted the time to do something meaningful in what seemed a self-consumed life. If time was a currency, I would say this was time well spent, despite it throwing up some limitations in my own character that you work through when caring for someone else's functional needs. Overall, I would say this experience made me more patient and kind; realising that you do not have long left to spend with people you hold dear has a way of sharply refocusing your priorities.

Once I finally realised that the private sector jobs I had been chasing ultimately felt like dead-ends since leaving my last role, I decided to shift gear. Following a suggestion from the head of my local employment office, I considered looking at public sector and charity focused jobs. This made perfect sense as what could be more meaningful than working in an area where you put the greater public need before the interests of shareholder profit? I routinely set about identifying suitable roles where I could transfer my skills in an effort to be successful in a different type of career. I engaged with a whole new world of possibility by looking at public sector and charity roles, feeling very buoyed up to know that there was another way forward. I would heartily recommend this as an alternative for those who still want to be gainfully employed, giving you the opportunity to align with a different set of values that ultimately serve the greater good.

My own journey did not stop here, however, as I couldn't shake the feeling that there was something else looking for my attention; even my daily journaling seemed to revolve around the theme of 'going it alone'. I strongly resonated with a feeling of being in charge of my own destiny, so to help me bottom this out, I applied for a Creativity & Innovation course to support me in the possibility of starting my own business. As the course was part-time, I could still work as a freelancer alongside it, knowing it would give me the opportunity to deep-dive on what life-enhancing business goals I could align myself with. Connecting with a like-minded cohort of people, all with their own organic business desires, provided a broader support net and a new network, filling the hole which now no longer seemed relevant or in tune with my current state of evolution.

Reflection

I did not have any idea where I would land when I heralded my own corp*exit*, however, know that there are alternative opportunities out there worth considering especially if you are truly unhappy with your current state of play. Your life *time* is too precious to squander on activity that does not help you to expand and evolve. You are more than what you settle for.

Task

If you were to consider your career alternatives, what skills would you wish to develop in yourself and what career activities would you happily leave behind? What career options would be of interest to you in the public sector, self-employment, charity work? What do you feel you would gain by pivoting to these opportunities?

CHAPTER 18

What I have learnt

In a word, I would say *well-being* has been the overwhelming benefit gained from my corp*exit*. Prior to that, I was stressed all the time. Even when I thought I was relaxing or taking a day off to tune out, the corporate culture deeply entrenched within my psyche was still there, running like a latent background process, continuously ebbing away at my life energy and life choices. Everything was coloured by what the corporate needed, from booking my 'free thought' time to the way I looked and valued the people and world around me. It was all done subconsciously through the corporate lens. Yes, I meditated the odd time, took yoga classes, joined a gym and tried to be mindful when I had the energy, but underpinning it all were the constraints that corporate life had imposed around my very existence and, in turn, that of my family. The ego may have been satisfied but the soul was starved to the point of invisibility, unvoiced, not permitted because the corporate price was that *your* key values aligned with *corporate* key values, and *your* behaviour and presentation to the world aligned with *corporate* behaviour and appearance.

We feel we are in control of our corporate experience by being *authentic in the workplace*, but really we are only permitting ourselves to being a fraction of our whole true selves when you really consider what your whole true self looks like and what it wants. The corporate you is a shallower projection of you, bent into a shape and way of being that meets the corporate brief and the acceptance of those operating within that sphere. When you step outside that way of being, only then can you fully permit yourself to follow your own path, only then can your own real aspirations and values surface. It is simply not possible to 'bring your whole self to work' when you are bound consciously and subconsciously by the overarching organisational need that, by its very nature, has to control its employees at some level to achieve its own goals. The corporate need can often be in direct conflict with your own soul need, so of course we learn to compromise, we condition ourselves to be and act in accordance with the organisation so we can fit in and, what's more, 'be successful' in the eyes of the corporate hierarchy. Bringing awareness to this trade-off we are making is necessary so we consciously understand what we are lacking as a result of our corporate buy-in and those aspects of our very being which are directly stunted as a result.

Looking back after a year outside corporate life, where I have endeavoured to piece together who I am at my very core now and own it with a view to *walking my own talk*, these are the things I feel I have received in return:

- I sleep peacefully at night
- I wake each morning without the previous unease that lay at the pit of my stomach each waking day due to alignment with my soul's need
- I no longer experience the weekend terrors, worrying

about what lay ahead on Monday morning

- I feel an excitement knowing that I am at last moving forward in my soul's experience
- I am so grateful for the peace I feel deep in my bones regardless of what challenges may occur in any given day (life still goes on, right; teens will still be teens, bills still arrive, people get sick, etc)
- I feel in control of my own destiny, no one making decisions on my behalf. I am sailing my own ship and fully accountable
- I have developed more meaningful relationships with my family and friends as I reach out beyond my previously limited life-range, expanding my horizons
- I enjoy my day more, each step has more value, is richer in hue because it is pure, organic and mine
- I am more conscientious about the environment and my CO^2 footprint
- I have lost weight due to less take-aways/eating out and more daily exercise
- I feel more connected with my community in a way I just did not have the time or energy for before which in turn is making life richer and more linked

Reflection

It is possible to retrieve your own true personal self and with it your soul's freedom to become what it is destined to become simply by altering why and how you do things, by approaching life from another angle that allows your true self to shine.

Task

What key benefits do you feel leaving your corporate life will bring you and your family? What would you like to achieve in your life if you were completely free to do anything your heart desired? What needs to change or start to enable you to start moving towards that desire?

What I miss about corporate life

There are a number of things I still do miss about corporate life:

- My corporate family – that group of smiling faces that you meet every single day, who are invested like you in keeping your corporate endeavours on the road, who are there when the s*1t is hitting the fan, and afterwards to support and dissect the details. As with any family, this is something that is really hard to replace when you are no longer part of the daily grind. The only way forward is to actively create or join new social groups, depending on your interests.

- The monthly pay-cheque – you only realise how very hard it is to piece together a modest living by yourself, having to chase down every single activity you can squeeze an income from when you compare it with the ease of simply receiving a standard pay cheque each month in lieu of your time, no questions asked.

- The bonus – the luxury of receiving a corporate bonus was something I had come to expect; in comparison, what I could do with a bonus now would mirror how I would feel if I were to win the lottery!

- Private medical cover – a luxury; need I say more?

- Getting paid for days off – as a freelancer, you need to carefully consider what time you take away from eking out your own living as no one is going to pay you for not being available to carry out contracted work.

- Going to work – oddly, I began to miss leaving the house to go to a place of work – just the act of being somewhere else, among different people who were all working on their own activities. As a substitute, I found a workspace in one of the many co-working units available and I have to say, it ticked the box for me. I even got to make the odd acquaintance at the space, even having idle chit-chat over the water cooler.

- Going out after work – Thursday was usually my favourite night for going out post-work, whether it was a few drinks with my corporate family or meeting my friends for dinner somewhere in town; this is something I still really miss.

- The social events that bring us all together, whether it was volunteering for the corporate's designated annual charity drive, meeting up with similar business folk or internal mentoring group meetings. These occasions were all ways of connecting with other people, doing similar things. Now I am no longer doing this I could easily feel like a bit of a loner, so I have started to eke out new voluntary activities with a blend of diverse groups, embracing new interests which all offer me the opportunity to actively build new social bonds (some of these include city meet-ups for innovation collaborators, my local running club or a myriad local volunteering and community groups).

- Lunch and trying new places – when lunchtime allowed, I

loved being able to try out new lunch spots using the time to meet up with colleagues, or even making use of a subsidised canteen. This is not something I do routinely anymore for financial reasons, however, the odd social coffee out feels like a true treat these days!

- Travel – in some of my corporate roles, I have had great opportunities to travel and I certainly miss that, even though most organisations will try to have you do everything online. Those work engagements where I have physically worked overseas have left indelible memories.

- Promotion and accolades – having people around you acknowledge your professional contribution, either through promotion or accolade, is an ego-boost and not something you can do for yourself.

What I do *not* miss

There are a number of prior work-related experiences which I am very happy to no longer continue:

- Spending 80% of my life's waking hours (and a significant portion of my sleep time dealing with the related work worries) by doing what I see now as an ultimately meaningless 'job' (sorry ego!), whose only benefit was lining the pockets of a few shady members of the wealthy elite, while trapping me in a money web where I main-lined salary as if it were cocaine, all the time evaluating my success in life by how much of the stuff I could accumulate.

- Work stress culminating from deadlines imposed on you and your team suddenly – oftentimes throughout corporate life, you can be asked to deliver to unrealistic deadlines based on commitments made without your input, e.g. regulatory changes, commitments made to external parties by sales, etc. These can have a seriously retrograde influence on the team's performance and your mental health.

- Corporate brainwashing/behavioural training – routine training episodes that are rolled out by HR groups telling you how you should think and act to be truly compliant in a corporate setting are, quite frankly, an infringement on your freedom of thought. These are carried out on such a frequent basis as to have the same effect as brain-washing.

- The endless need to make your and your team's work visible in a sea of global employees so that you can acquire funding, gain notoriety for your endeavours, groom those above you for your ascension up the greasy pole.

- The need for you to trawl through literally thousands of unrelated work mails daily so you can isolate the few key *need to know* items is a perpetual waste of time.

- Having to massage your superior's ego while you work your ass off to ensure that all ducks are in row and optimally armed every day.

- Being on vacation and trying to switch off from all the work items you know you have to go back to soon …

- Getting up at the crack of dawn to ensure the pumps are all still working, wade through the mail, get ahead of any fire-fighting, then continuing online for another 12 hours.

- The fire drills that come out of nowhere, usually on a Friday evening just before you are set to logoff for the day, with work that needs to be done right there and then by you or your team.

- That little light that goes from green to red, showing you are 'away from your PC' to go to the loo, feed your kids, stave off a panic attack, etc.

- The brown-nosers, sucking up to you, your boss and their boss and their boss.

- Those that are looking to shamelessly take the credit for the sweat and toil by work actually done by you/your team.

- The lack of opportunity for you to really drive the changes your group needs because no one wants to shake the tree above too much for fear of falling out of favour with the tree gods.

- The corporate tree gods and their relentless updates on how wonderful a job they are doing, the brown-nosing with other tree gods to ensure they are seen as the wonderful superior beings they truly are. My advice: level the forest as those green shoots need sunlight to grow.

- The drama queens/bullies (you know who they are in your organisation) who have the power to kill your funding, your overworked team's drive and your team's work-life balance because they have just thrown their toys out of the pram realising they can't have what they've just decided they want ASAP!

- ASAP – I hope I never have to use or work to that phrase ever again – *fail to plan, plan to fail.*

CHAPTER 19

Things to consider before jumping in with both feet

I have mentioned the very real impact this decision will have on you and those around you, as well as your finances. Here are some things to consider before taking the plunge:

- Get some clarity on your primary motivations for the change (why you want it), such as:
  - Looking to learn new life skills or dig deeper into working with your hobbies
  - Looking for flexibility in your schedule
  - Desiring to be your own boss
  - Wanting to change location, e.g. A move to the country, a change of country

- Save as much as you can in advance of your exit; a minimum of six months' salary should help to ease the initial blow and give you room to think. Even six months passes quickly when you are giving yourself time to change, so consider the other financial exercises I mention in the chapter 'Doing the Math'.

- If you have already identified a potential business idea or career transition that you would like to pursue, then consider doing one of the following before you make the leap to get an insider perspective and help you clarify your motives for change:

- Volunteering in your chosen field
- Taking part-time/weekend work doing the actual job
- Taking a sabbatical or a leave of absence/parental leave to give yourself a trial run at your new life before closing the door on the old

- Putting a loose time frame around your transition with some high-level goals for yourself is a good idea from the outset so you don't end up drifting. You will find that new goals surface as you progress on your journey but having something you can check in on every six months is a way of grounding you and perhaps challenging you to create some shape and direction around your activities.

- To give yourself the maximum chance of creating a clear canvas for your new creative process, I would encourage you to tune out the media, reading and any other similar activity that consumes your energy for a time – of course, if you need to read/go online to research ideas, that is a positive way of using your energy but just be wary of taking in unnecessary information. We are awash with information now and often become clogged up creatively as a result. This is a time of birthing a new version of yourself so literally storing up your energy for your highest and best outcomes is critical.

- In a similar vein, be careful with whom you choose to share your ideas and plans; everyone will see things differently and some of the more negative responses may detract from the bubble of optimistic energy you need to surround yourself with. I only shared my ideas and observations with my partner, who had my best interests at heart, and just a handful of close friends. I was acutely aware of how other people's expectations could put pressure on achieving 'the right outcome' so I refrained as much as possible from sharing, especially when I had no real idea what was happening in those early days. It is always surprising to see how some people that you may consider to have your best interests responding in a way you would never have suspected, some quite negatively, as if you had somehow put their whole field of values into question. At this juncture, it is best to leave life-limiting agendas until you are well beyond the cocoon stage. You may initially feel quite fragile/sensitive/vulnerable as you shed your old skin; this is all absolutely normal and those tips I suggested for bringing TLC into your life (see chapter 'Assembling a Toolbox') will help you maintain a sphere of openness to possibility which is critical for positive life opportunity to reach you.

Reflection

Ultimately, the process of change you invoke into your life by taking this decision can yield a period of turmoil if you jump in wholly unprepared. Laying out some loose plans around timing, finances and high-level goals can offer some stability as you enter a state of flux.

Task

What steps would you need to take to enable you to test the waters on your corp*exit*? Can you put a loose time frame around these steps? Who in your life would offer positive support while giving you space to change? Do you see any immediate blockers? What can you do to work around them?

CHAPTER 20

Imagining a new future of work

It is easy to get bogged down in pointing out what is wrong with the current corporate sphere, however, I think we owe it to ourselves and the salaries we need to sustain ourselves to imagine what a different future in corporate-land would look like if the broader human agenda was put ahead of shareholder needs. This is not an exercise I can take on alone; after all, many minds create more broadly imagined possibilities, so I have enlisted other workers and also a younger cohort who have yet to join the world of work to help shape what their ideal future working model could look like.

What strikes us first is the need to address the imbalance of corporate profit that is currently directed to a handful of shareholders – this power balance needs to be addressed from the outset and needs to be done globally, all at once, so we end the inequality of one jurisdiction treating workers more unfairly than in others. If we change the game together, we can raise the stakes and improve life for us all – we all deserve a better outcome here.

Putting work in its place

Since the middle-ages, the meaning of work stemmed from a form of indentured service or enslavement in order that agricultural work predominantly would get done for the landowners and the Church (some might say it still feels like enslavement of sorts today but we'll leave that for another discussion). Over the centuries, the type of work people 'do' has expanded with increasing global trade and the industrial revolution under our belts. We are in the midst of a technology revolution which is supposed to aid us by moving humanity's capabilities forward, possibly superseding humanity if AI is permitted to take over.

Setting this aside, if we look at today's society and how the notion of what work *is* has evolved, it is something that is done in exchange for money. If you are running your own business, working for the public service or a charity in a non-volunteering capacity or, indeed, like the bulk of humanity, working for a corporate, then this transaction of money for your time holds true. Always in society we have had the artists, those blessed with a divine set of gifts whether it be art, writing poetry or creating music or dance. These arty folk are often viewed as the lucky few whose life-path was almost pre-destined and whose art is their work (though understanding how challenging it can be to make a living this way may counter the blessing somewhat).

But what about the rest of us who may not be so overtly blessed with such talents? What of our life path, when we don't actually know quite what we are really good at or how we can best add to or develop our value in society? Yes, with age comes wisdom and along your life-path you can pick out the skills you have honed at that point in time (see the Skills Tool in Appendix A to help you work out yours!). My question to you is whether you are really thinking big enough or do you find yourself blinkered by your economic value, seeing yourself only through the lens of your success in the working sphere? Could there be more in your make-up than you are currently aware of, gifts which lie latent because all of your life energy is being usurped to eke that working wage? The truth is that many of us will never reach our full potential, though if you are blessed to live in a free, democratic society then you have the chance at least to discover more about yourself, if you deign to. For some this will seem too nebulous or too far out of reach, requiring too much energy to shift gear from just working and getting paid in return to taking some time out to figure out what you really are about.

Find out the meaning of your existence by looking inward to try and understand who you really are outside of the way society or your family and friends see you. If you were entirely free from all the masks and could be shamelessly yourself for a day, what would you choose to do? Shift your idea of work towards those skills that you actually want to grow or learn (not just out of corporate necessity but your actual desire to try something because it holds some fascination for you), thereby giving you the opportunity to broaden your horizons, making work something you desire rather than simply a thing you have to do because you have exchanged your soul for a pay cheque, status or a comfy office.

I do not suggest this lightly; I understand that we are constantly trying to balance our soul search with being able to meet our basic survival needs. At the same time, though, we should not guide our whole lives to just putting food on the table or keeping up with the Joneses, but rather look beyond the material and aspire to add that extra bit of spice to our life. There is no doubt that having a universal basic income to fall back on would help us address the fear of not having money to meet these basic needs, especially when we are considering making a life transition that may take some time to work through then bedding down the changes in our lives. It would stop us holding on so tightly to those work choices that no longer serve us well, avoiding the obvious health impact and cost of falling into the arms of depression or chronic disease that stem from continuing to put our life energy into a job that feels ultimately meaningless in the grand scheme of our lives and does not align with our core life values.

Step out of the rut and decide to listen to yourself, really listen to what you want to 'do', thus feeling empowered enough to make a plan of how you might be able to balance the needs of your true self with the demands of your earthly existence.

Imagine if you could get up every day and carry out the things you enjoy doing whilst balancing it with your and your family's needs, but not letting it eat up your full quota of life energy so you end up too wrecked to even contemplate doing anything that might nourish yourself. Some of you may operate from this space already but for most, achieving that balance can be seen as an insurmountable challenge. Carving out even a little time for soul nourishment at first is the first step towards meeting the *potential* you, the best version of you – so why wait? I encourage you to start your adventure today;

do it knowing that you call the shots in your own life, that you are in control, that you have the choice – and if you really want to transform and bloom, you can and will.

Sharing a significant portion of corporate profit with our communities

By making it mandatory for all corporates to make our communities significant shareholders, we can change the balance of power. This new shareholder voting voice will in itself start to form a better outcome. The community benefits would be staggering in terms of accelerating research and provision of improved healthcare, infrastructure and environmental development; ultimately, it could improve the lives of people everywhere, raising the standard for all. Why should one small group of people siphon off all the wealth? It's not equitable nor in the human interest to have a few shadowy figures pulling the strings of our economies, and indeed our human futures, while the rest of us play the slave game as we fight to keep our heads above water; things have to change here. Telling us that AI will replace our jobs but those on high will bestow on us a living wage just isn't going to be enough; the corporate elite need to understand that we also want to be empowered to steer the course of our human future alongside the one or two wealthy families that have been living off our toil for centuries – it's time to turn the table here so we can give our children a world to be excited about and that they want to be a part of as equal citizens and inheritors of the earth and its many resources. We need to call time on the race to the pit we now find ourselves frazzled by just because a group of elite profiteers want more from us, driven by their own insane greed for more power and dominance over us workers.

We need to remember that *we* are the governments in our world; *we* may elect specific candidates to voice our opinions but it is just that – *our* opinions, *our* desires, *our* needs, *our* will – so shifting the flow of money to water the ground for us all, rather than just the few, has to be our next course of action. It's insane not to advocate for this. What other reason would there be for keeping things the way they are today? What benefit does it bring to the human race? We need to tune out the bray of the nay-sayers and media spinners, who do not wish for change because they do not have our best interests at heart and who most likely are entirely comfortable in their lives. They don't feel anything should change or they just can't imagine that things really can change so, but for the rest of us, we could start to dream and innovate collectively, organisations would evolve organically and meet a shared vision, not just the basic mantra of *more, more, more* that the elite are driving us into the ground for. Just imagine what our community and environment would look like with this shift in gear …

Changing the working environment

We typically tend to work in sterile, grey, artificially lit square or rectangular boxes. Like factory hens, we toil in these conditions for the vast majority of our waking hours. Working from home is a welcome natural break from this clinical environment we are being forced back into as companies suggest more collaboration is needed to improve company productivity, even though most of our global teams are now located in different countries, thus our screens are a more realistic means of collaboration. When we imagine what a beautiful, natural feeling shared work space might look like, it is a far more distant vision than what we are presented with today.

Imagine if you could collaborate in an environment surrounded by plants, purified air and water, in large light-filled domes not unlike the Eden Project in Cornwall which embraces the use of low-energy, geodesic, and architecture inspired by nature designed by Sir Nicholas Grimshaw? Grimshaw also redesigned the international terminal at London's Waterloo Station. He says: *I have always felt we should use the technology of the age we live in for the improvement of mankind.'*

'The moment we saw it we loved it, because it felt natural, a biological response to our needs, but forged in materials that would allow us to explore the cultivation of plants in a way never before attempted.' (Ref edenproject.com)

Imagine structures that allow fresh, invigorated air to flow, with natural light and nature including trees, waterfalls, rocks, etc, all bringing to you the natural environment we desire to escape to when we get stressed but rarely get to; spherical or organic-shaped structures all connecting, with access to all the services humans need including parks, fitness/well-being centres, schools/creches, shopping and public transport all fully integrated into 'the domes'. What a transcendental experience that could be! How the stresses would ebb away with the ease and energy release you achieve from just being in a natural space and being able to get to the ones you love quickly! How easy it might be to network and collaborate even if it's raining; how enlivened we all might feel by communising in this way; how different our cities might feel as a result as they, too, evolve to integrate with this strange new landscape and architecture.

Hot-desking has been driven across corporates as the squeeze for seating apparently becomes an issue, effectively dehumanizing the working space (despite being left with the uglier remnants of your predecessors such as bacteria, nails, chewed pen tops, spillages ... should I go on?). I remember one company I worked for years back, before the dehumanizing started, where a worker with quite a gregarious personality had his desk kitted out with a plethora of family photographs, a pink feather boa, a collection of funny little animal statues that he collected and added to over the years — the desk reflected him completely and I am sure he felt quite at home as he landed there each day ... however, when the Nothing came (reference *The NeverEnding Story*, the 80's film that turns fertile fields into desert) and vanquished his space, I can imagine it was like a beautiful bright light being extinguished. I can't imagine he liked going to work as much after that. As humans, we are, underneath our stylish clothes, coifs and makeup, still ultimately animals and, like animals who are known to go back to the exact same place in their barns every day, we are fundamentally the same: we like routine, we like what is ours, we like our nest to look a certain way. What we do not typically like is clinical, grey, hot-desks that change every day — this does not make humans feel secure or cared for, and as a result we cannot deliver beyond average in these bland, working environments.

Changing the *way* we work

Today, working as an employee in a large corporate can feel like a very controlled experience: you get through the barrier at work, you find your hot-desk or, if working from home, you just log-in and immediately you are under some level of surveillance. Next comes the flood of mail, IMs, meetings, slack and workflow, and so the work day begins for many employees where the first few hours of work at least will be spent just catching up.

Every move online is tracked by the watchful eye of that little indicator that even after five minutes away from your desk can change to 'Away'. You may be away for some time if you're at work meetings, talking to colleagues, doing workshops, in the toilet, etc but the reality is that the little light alerts all workers that you are being watched. Of course, there are more detailed methods of surveillance going on aside from when you clock in and clock out, how much time you spend actively online, which applications you use and for how long and how much you write, whether it be words or code; all data points are captured and routinely checked against thresholds to determine if Employee A is being as productive as the organisation expects, and if not, it's a point of evaluation in the performance review process.

From a McKinsey report, it appears that the average professional worker spends over a quarter of their workday reading and answering mail.

https://www.mckinsey.com/industries/technology-media-and-telecommunications/our-insights/the-social-economy (Ref 13/09/2023)

In some work situations, I have felt that it can sometimes be way more. From my own experience I could literally spend all day in mail, reading, reacting and keeping up with the work community around me – the problem is that everyone gets caught up in the maelstrom of being seen, being heard, participating actively on mail, because it is expected. Mail is much more than just passively reading something that has reached your inbox and, if the mood takes you or the need is evident, responding to it. Mail is routinely used as a way to get tacit agreement on things as trivial as where the team may go for lunch, to more pernicious use where, for example, it can demand group digestion and immediate response on, very often, quite complex themes that should be handled elsewhere in dedicated conversation threads between key participants to work through the topic at hand in a methodical and time-permitting manner.

These mails can be sent to tens, hundreds or even thousands of people depending on how big your business cohort is, requiring everyone from the highest ranking down to be included, then someone responds and another and another, telling them to stop responding and so it goes on. Another waste of air-time. Worse still are the threads that request input or try to achieve a consensus for often quite complex topics, with everyone, particularly the SMEs, expected to share their immediate view, whether it be on the latest market trends, compliance issues, client concerns, regulatory insight, product changes, technical or business queries, or to help address one person's gap in understanding. These often end up as one big chain mail where people are commenting on other comments as well as giving their own views, with no clear outcome at the end of the thread unless you are willing to scroll through all the highlights, which I have had to do many times to understand what the consensus view point is. All of this mail interaction repeated over and over again oils the turbines of the company's key decision-making, demanding the full attention of everyone on the 'to' and 'cc' lists and is a highly unproductive approach to acquiring feedback or input that would be better done in a composed, considered way; not off the cuff because 'that's all you have time for' given the pressurised focus on getting the responses. Worse still, these chains can be invoked by just about anyone, everyone paranoid that they don't miss their moment to respond before the boss sets eyes on it so that it spikes employees' stress levels, especially if they are already handling their daily workload whilst flapping through a work crisis in the background.

Not only does mail detract from the workers' concentration, only to be broken when they are embedded in one of the many physical or online meetings (even then, during meetings you can see people's eyes flicker as they continuously scan emails on screen as if their working life depended on it, all in an effort to keep up with the latest), it is like one long running meeting during your day that only at your peril will you leave. Yes, you may get away with lunch if colleagues step away from their screens, but there are still many who will not leave their screen, let alone their desks, just in case they miss something big that needs immediate attention.

It is rare with all the reacting and show-ponying to get real time to digest things fully; more often than not the response is demanded instantaneously so you furtively scan your mail to eke out the salient points for debate or resolution so that you can respond in what is often a very large, highly visible forum where if you put one foot wrong, your credibility is on the line. In my view, this is a terrible way to run a complex organisation: not only are you forcing your workforce to use most of their creative hours perusing mail of which at least 70% is going to be absolutely irrelevant to them, you are continuously expecting your workforce to spit-ball responses to complex elements of key decisions (who is not doing what they should be doing here that it requires a group of sometimes 100 to be mailed to input on a topic that only a few SMEs should need to handle). Not only are organisations then distracting the main body of the workforce from the job that you hired them for in the first place, the small handful of SMEs and senior managers are bombarded to respond in quick-fire fashion as if they have been trapped in a never-ending *Mastermind* challenge – and we wonder why people burnout? Some will argue that this is a necessary part of the job, but think about it: if you can eliminate a large cohort of people from reading at least 70% of their email because it literally has no direct impact on them or no need for their input then you are giving them back vital time to get productive work done. Then they can focus on what is being asked and how that can be dealt with in a more organised manner, allowing them to engage when they have time in their diary, rather than reacting. Redirect the meaty themes as tasks that need to be solved. I would prefer a passive form of communication channel such as Slack or a Jira-style task, complete with workflow and ranking, so I know who has read the ask prior to me, when it needs to be done by and which allows me the time and space to work through the latest list of asks in a scheduled, methodical way. Giving more diary time to digesting complex themes ensures improved quality in our responses, lower risk of fallout and a more structured way of collating and validating data which has to be better than the race to compete with 'who can respond the fastest' on email.

Yes, you can create mail filters in your mailbox to weed out the generic bulletins, mail-chains, updates, etc. However, mail is often used more insidiously than that; by including your name directly, you are obliged to open the mail to check it for value. Routinely every morning I would spend at least 1-2 hours scanning the hundreds of mails that awaited my attention, deleting those of no interest, moving those of lesser importance (which the mail filter could not pick up), placing them in a bunch of work folders which I ranked based on priority, all with the single intention of ending up with the handful of mails that actually needed my immediate attention. These I would deal with first and from there I worked through the ranked folders or whatever pressing instant messages, slack, meetings, Jiras needed me next.

All these tools divvy up the guts of online work; the problem is that all are expected to be responded to ASAP, ad nauseam. No wonder workers get stressed – this never-ending cycle of dealing with the competing communication channels never actually gives the worker any creative down-time.

There are many multi-tasking tools which bring all the channels together in one place in a neat dashboard, but all the channels and competing tasks can end up bombarding workers – multi-tasking, according to a Stanford neuroscience study, can do more harm than good; in fact, the research suggests that it is less efficient to do two or more tasks at the same time, rather the human brain is better at focusing on the completion of one task at a sustained time. Multi-tasking can have a detrimental impact on our memory by causing interference with the brain's processing during a single task. So, the next time you feel you are being super efficient at dealing with multiple tasks, think again at the impact on yourself, both in the moment and long-term to your memory and its ability to process.

https://www.neuroscience.stanford.edu/news/why-multitasking-does-more-harm-good (Accessed 14 September 2023)

We need a fresh approach to work and I don't mean making it more super-efficient. I think corporates have squeezed enough out of the worker, thank you! People like to add value, we like to feel we can add our own creative mark, and if we are not permitted to be creative during our workday, there is no doubt that we will start to disengage, becoming more robotic at just filling the time. But at this point management should listen up – productivity will take a nose-dive. If you would like to change things for your workforce, empowering people and enabling active conversation has to be more conducive to providing the green-space for innovation and performance to thrive, and, most importantly, follow-through. There is nothing more demotivating than lip-service with no follow-up. Do what you say you are going to do, then the worker will know that at least they are working in an authentically caring work environment, and if not, well they can and will leave.

So, in changing the way we work from the over-wrought

'now, now, now' reactivity present in a lot of organisations that continually put workers under ridiculous pressure to stay on top of the plethora of communication channels (mail, workflow, IMs, meetings, Jiras etc) whilst trying to get the day job done, we need to change the style and expectation around the interaction replacing the endless drills with a steady, even flow that the worker feels they have some control over and can work through sequentially.

In a more utopic work existence, we cite a means to earning a living that is not dominating our very existence as it is today. We work 8-10 hours per day of on average 14 waking hours in fact! Work simply needs to be curtailed: five hours per day is now being suggested as the optimum number of working hours to both improve productivity and our overall well-being.

Work also needs to be flexible enough to fit in with our more meaningful life activities so that life comes first and work second, not the other way around as it does for most of us today.

We want a work day that is organic and fluid and evenly balanced, but keeps us interested, energised and gives us the opportunity to step outside in nature and breathe. We need to look at replacing today's toxic corporate culture of reaction to one of mindful interaction with clearly defined no-contact zones to help freshen everyone's perspective, sharpening our mental processing power and allowing some creative innovation to seed itself amongst the daily grind, overall allowing for a healthier and more productive workforce to thrive in organically appointed spaces both at home and in collaboration when it is needed. We want to create a world where our children can aspire to one day joining us in carrying out the many activities that are necessitated in keeping us humans healthy, fed and watered whilst removing those activities that are today carried out at other workers' expense, e.g. sweat shops and factories creating non-sustainable, dispensable, single-use products that are to no one's long-term benefit. Everyone deserves the opportunity to work creatively and be part of an equally healthy working environment; this is not just a privilege for the sacrosanct few.

A high tide lifts all boats, so we need to do this together.

Reflection

If we continue to work as a species, then we need to change the dynamic, i.e. how we approach work, who benefits from our work, ensuring our society receives a material benefit with full transparency around who is getting what and why, how we collaborate, how we balance work with our lives and desires and abilities, how we can make every worker feel worthwhile and acknowledged while also enabling people to feel they can move around, re-train, grow, take time out when they need it without feeling like an indentured servant. There are many fine minds out there who can contribute toward a global charter for working and what that means in an evolved society. No longer can workers be seen as those just grubbing along to get a pay cheque – we want to be active participants in how our world is run. The global financial economy needs to be rethought and rebuilt to ensure that wealth is distributed fairly across society and that no one group of individuals holds the voting power to chart the course of humanity, particularly when it works against our needs. We strive to be active conscious beings that want to have a say in how things are run at all levels; we no longer want to be mushrooms (you know the line – mushrooms sit in the dark and are fed bullsh** all day long). As a consequence, the way our world is run has to change, those shadow controllers need to move over because the future is here, we are awakening from our work-induced comas, and know this: humanity will not settle for less than what our human civilisation needs to ensure a truly equitable, honest and fair society for all.

Task

What bright new way of working do you dream of? What changes would you like to see?

APPENDIX A

Workbook

Why not buy your own journal and dedicate time each week to working through the following tasks that are covered in each of the preceding chapters:

Your own work journey task

Draw up your own career journey to date (using a line graph in PowerPoint is the simplest way to do this). What does it tell you about your journey so far?

What pivots may be necessary for your growth and ease?

When looks like a good time to take your first step?

Leaving the cult

Reviewing the cult-like tendencies, are any of these at play in your current work organisation?

What steps can you take to protect your own ingenuity and credibility?

A slow release

What are you undertaking in your work life that makes you feel unhappy and what can you do to alleviate it?

What would happen if you simply *let go*? Write out the impacts and benefits to clarify for yourself.

Closing the door

What do you imagine the blockers to leaving your current corporate space might be? Take note of any feelings attached to these blockers.

What mindset will help you to override those feelings to enable you move forward?

The roller-coaster

What does your ego cling to, to keep your world 'safe' and harmonious?

What feels unsafe to you, and why?

What might happen if you override your ego?

Maybe Maslow had it right?

Looking at Maslow's hierarchy of needs, which do you feel you resonate with the most right now?

What are you looking for here or what do you feel you need?

What steps do you need to take to meet that need?

Where do you feel you are currently on the cycle of transformation? Note that even if you are still considering getting off the starting block, at least you are there challenging yourself to what may come next!

Assembling a toolbox

What relaxes you and helps you to unwind (beyond the odd glass of wine!)? How often do you afford yourself the time to take pleasure in doing the things you love?

Do you think you could make a date with yourself on a regular basis to take time for your own enjoyment? Even if it's an hour a week, it will be an hour that is yours, a true gift to yourself to acknowledge that yes, you are special, and yes, you do deserve this.

Do the math

What would you do with your time if your basic needs were taken care of?

Where would you want to focus your interest?

Identify steps to create a bridge to that interest from where you are in your life right now, e.g. identify a course or voluntary activity that could let you try out your area of interest without having to make a sudden leap.

Understanding why we work

Think about what work means to you – does it offer you what you need? What would you choose to do if work as we know it ceased to exist?

How corporates function

If you have any takeaways or light-bulb moments after reading this section, record them now along with any meaningful actions you wish to take.

Corporate burnout:

What stressors are apparent within your workplace and what steps, if any, can you take to address them? For example, discuss with HR, your boss, your colleagues, launch an initiative to bring visibility to it? What personal action can you take to aid your own well-being?

Family impact

How do you think your nearest and dearest will react to your change of course?

What ways will it specifically impact them and what would your response be to. those impacts?

Is there an opportunity for growth and change in your family circle as a result of your action?

How might it benefit you all in the long run?

Sacrifice

What are your non-compromisable lifestyle priorities? What could you learn to do without?

Is there an opportunity for changing your lifestyle to a more optimal model that better serves your needs longer term? What might that optimal life model look like for you?

What steps would you need to take to start moving towards that new way of living?

What benefits do you think might come from the change?

Toxic quirks

What toxic quirks do you feel it would serve you well to stop so that you can enter your next chapter without shame or judgment, to ensure you are a blank canvas, open to all possibility?

Life a year on

If you were to consider your career alternatives, what skills would you wish to develop in yourself and what career activities would you happily leave behind?

What other career options would be of interest to you in the private sector? Also consider opportunities in the public sector, self-employment, charity work.

What do you feel you would gain by pivoting to these

opportunities?

What key benefits do you feel exiting your current corporate life will bring you and your family?

What would you like to achieve in your life if you were completely free to do anything your heart desired?

What needs to change or start to enable you to start moving towards that desire?

Things to consider before jumping in:

What steps you need to take before jumping in with both feet

What steps would you need to take to enable you to test the waters on your corp*exit*?

Can you put a loose time frame around these steps?

Who in your life would offer positive support while giving you space to change?

Do you see any immediate blockers? What can you do to work around them?

Imagining a new future

What bright new way of working do you dream of? What changes would you like to see?

APPENDIX B

Shining a light on your skills

By taking time to complete this easy exercise, you can identify which life/work skills you seek to hone or ditch by working out your personal motivations. Set an hour or two aside (somewhere quiet so you can get right down to it) and choose whether you want to use a pen and paper, a whiteboard, an Excel sheet or Word table on your computer. It may help to talk it through after with a friend or partner but most important of all is to let your instinct guide you; leave your functional mind at the door, please.

Step 1

Draw up your table with top line headings along the lines of the following (feel free to make up your own!):

- Love doing this!

- Like this and find myself doing it regularly

- Like this, wish I could do it more though

- Dislike this, it's blah blah

- To say I hate this is an understatement

Down the side of your table, create these four headings with plenty of space underneath each one:

- Total expert at this

- Good at this, feel capable doing it

- Needs work or training to improve

- Complete disaster at this

It should look something like this:

	Love Doing this!	Like this and do it regularly	Like this, wish I could do it more often	Dislike this	To say I hate doing this is an understatement
Total Expert at this					
Total Expert at this					
Total Expert at this					
Total Expert at this					
Good at this, feel capable doing it					
Good at this, feel capable doing it					
Good at this, feel capable doing it					
Good at this, feel capable doing it					
Good at this, feel capable doing it					
Good at this, feel capable doing it					
Good at this, feel capable doing it					
Good at this, feel capable doing it					
Needs work or training to improve					
Needs work or training to improve					
Needs work or training to improve					
Complete disaster at this					

Step 2

Starting with **Love doing this / Total expert at this,** fill in all the skills you feel resonate with this.

For example: I love gardening and consider myself a real boffin on the subject.

Next do the same under each heading until you have filled out the table completely.

Here is an example of what it may look like, filled with your own preferences of course:

	Love Doing this!	Like this and do it regularly	Like this, wish I could do it more often	Dislike this	To say I hate doing this is an understatement
Total Expert at this	Planning	Coming up with new ideas	Working with spreadsheets	Managing Time	Record Keeping
Total Expert at this	Innovating	Meeting and making friends	Nature conservation	Multi-tasking	Entertaining/Performing
Total Expert at this	Saving money	Cooking	Evaluating	Monitoring	
Total Expert at this	Gardening	Adaptability	Making Decisions	Coordinating	
Good at this, feel capable doing it	Drawing	Meditating	Supervising	Using Technology	
Good at this, feel capable doing it	Designing	Innovating	Volunteering		
Good at this, feel capable doing it	Coordinating events	Cleaning up	Liasing	Editing	Testing
Good at this, feel capable doing it	Teaching / Training	Analysing	Team working	Implementing	
Good at this, feel capable doing it		Leading	Observing	Expediting	
Good at this, feel capable doing it		Delegating	Budgeting		
Good at this, feel capable doing it		Mediating	Writing		
Needs work or training to improve		Mentoring	Mechanical		
Needs work or training to improve		Yoga	Managing Change		
Needs work or training to improve	Counselling/Coaching	Negotiating	Creating online content	Dealing with Public criticism	Selling
Needs work or training to improve			Researching	Making things up	
Complete disaster at this				Sport activities	

Step 3

Now it's time to deep-dive into what your table is telling you, so grab a notepad or use your computer and get ready to make some lists, jotting down each of the headings:

My preferences – jot down the entries from your **Love doing this** or **Like this and do it regularly** paired with the **Total expert** or **Good at this** rows in your table. So, using the example above, it would mean you arrive at the highlighted area:

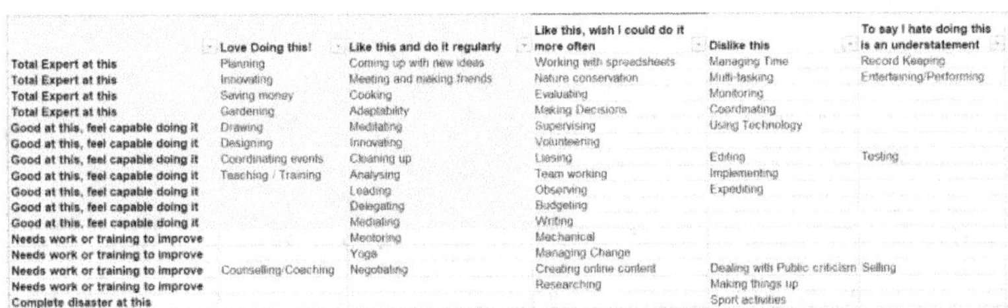

	Love Doing this!	Like this and do it regularly	Like this, wish I could do it more often	Dislike this	To say I hate doing this is an understatement
Total Expert at this	Planning	Coming up with new ideas	Working with spreadsheets	Managing Time	Record Keeping
Total Expert at this	Innovating	Meeting and making friends	Nature conservation	Multi-tasking	Entertaining/Performing
Total Expert at this	Saving money	Cooking	Evaluating	Monitoring	
Total Expert at this	Gardening	Adaptability	Making Decisions	Coordinating	
Good at this, feel capable doing it	Drawing	Meditating	Supervising	Using Technology	
Good at this, feel capable doing it	Designing	Innovating	Volunteering		
Good at this, feel capable doing it	Coordinating events	Cleaning up	Liesing	Editing	Testing
Good at this, feel capable doing it	Teaching / Training	Analysing	Team working	Implementing	
Good at this, feel capable doing it		Leading	Observing	Expediting	
Good at this, feel capable doing it		Delegating	Budgeting		
Good at this, feel capable doing it		Mediating	Writing		
Needs work or training to improve		Mentoring	Mechanical		
Needs work or training to improve		Yoga	Managing Change		
Needs work or training to improve	Counselling/Coaching	Negotiating	Creating online content	Dealing with Public criticism	Selling
Needs work or training to improve			Researching	Making things up	
Complete disaster at this				Sport activities	

Your preferences point to the things you enjoy, like to talk about or share with others. These are the skills your future you wants to keep using.

My areas of potential and growth

Jot down the entries from your **Love doing this** or **Like this and do it regularly** paired with the **Needs work or training to improve** row.

Using the example above would mean you arrive at the highlighted area:

	Love Doing this!	Like this and do it regularly	Like this, wish I could do it more often	Dislike this	To say I hate doing this is an understatement
Total Expert at this	Planning	Coming up with new ideas	Working with spreadsheets	Managing Time	Record Keeping
Total Expert at this	Innovating	Meeting and making friends	Nature conservation	Multi-tasking	Entertaining/Performing
Total Expert at this	Saving money	Cooking	Evaluating	Monitoring	
Total Expert at this	Gardening	Adaptability	Making Decisions	Coordinating	
Good at this, feel capable doing it	Drawing	Meditating	Supervising	Using Technology	
Good at this, feel capable doing it	Designing	Innovating	Volunteering		
Good at this, feel capable doing it	Coordinating events	Cleaning up	Liasing	Editing	Testing
Good at this, feel capable doing it	Teaching / Training	Analysing	Team working	Implementing	
Good at this, feel capable doing it		Leading	Observing	Expediting	
Good at this, feel capable doing it		Delegating	Budgeting		
Good at this, feel capable doing it		Mediating	Writing		
Needs work or training to improve		Mentoring	Mechanical		
Needs work or training to improve		Yoga	Managing Change		
Needs work or training to improve	Counselling/Coaching	Negotiating	Creating online content	Dealing with Public criticism Selling	
Needs work or training to improve			Researching	Making things up	
Complete disaster at this				Sport activities	

Areas of potential and growth are the things we enjoy doing (our green shoots) which just need some encouragement and development. Working on learning more about these skills will not only make you happy as you strengthen new facets within your life, but you will be more motivated to do these as they steer you towards new opportunities and expand your life journey.

My worn patches

Jot down the entries from your **Dislike this, it's blah blah / To say I hate this is an understatement** paired with **Total expert at this.**

You may be surprised by what you find here; this is a list of skills you would have enjoyed using at one time but due to continuously doing them or overdoing them, you now can't stand using them any longer (like that once favourite sweater that you wore daily and realise you can't stand the sight of, so really you need to stop wearing it or just put it to the back of the cupboard so you can rediscover it in a year or two – or maybe never).

Using the example, this would mean you arrive at the highlighted entries:

	Love Doing this!	Like this and do it regularly	Like this, wish I could do it more often	Dislike this	To say I hate doing this is an understatement
Total Expert at this	Planning	Coming up with new ideas	Working with spreadsheets	Managing Time	Record Keeping
Total Expert at this	Innovating	Meeting and making friends	Nature conservation	Multi-tasking	Entertaining/Performing
Total Expert at this	Saving money	Cooking	Evaluating	Monitoring	
Total Expert at this	Gardening	Adaptability	Making Decisions	Coordinating	
Good at this, feel capable doing it	Drawing	Meditating	Supervising	Using Technology	
Good at this, feel capable doing it	Designing	Innovating	Volunteering		
Good at this, feel capable doing it	Coordinating events	Cleaning up	Liasing	Editing	Testing
Good at this, feel capable doing it	Teaching / Training	Analysing	Team working	Implementing	
Good at this, feel capable doing it		Leading	Observing	Expediting	
Good at this, feel capable doing it		Delegating	Budgeting		
Good at this, feel capable doing it		Mediating	Writing		
Needs work or training to improve		Mentoring	Mechanical		
Needs work or training to improve		Yoga	Managing Change		
Needs work or training to improve	Counselling/Coaching	Negotiating	Creating online content	Dealing with Public criticism	Selling
Needs work or training to improve			Researching	Making things up	
Complete disaster at this				Sport activities	

Continuing to do this right now is life-inhibiting as it drains your energy even though you are really, really good at it. The advice is: *Use only sparingly, if at all!*

My ditch-list

Jot down the entries from your **To say I hate this is an understatement** paired with **Needs work or training to improve** or **Complete disaster at this.**

Using the example, it would mean ditching the highlighted entries, so no more selling for me!

	Love Doing this!	Like this and do it regularly	Like this, wish I could do it more often	Dislike this	To say I hate doing this is an understatement
Total Expert at this	Planning	Coming up with new ideas	Working with spreadsheets	Managing Time	Record Keeping
Total Expert at this	Innovating	Meeting and making friends	Nature conservation	Multi-tasking	Entertaining/Performing
Total Expert at this	Saving money	Cooking	Evaluating	Monitoring	
Total Expert at this	Gardening	Adaptability	Making Decisions	Coordinating	
Good at this, feel capable doing it	Drawing	Meditating	Supervising	Using Technology	
Good at this, feel capable doing it	Designing	Innovating	Volunteering		
Good at this, feel capable doing it	Coordinating events	Cleaning up	Liasing	Editing	Testing
Good at this, feel capable doing it	Teaching / Training	Analysing	Team working	Implementing	
Good at this, feel capable doing it		Leading	Observing	Expediting	
Good at this, feel capable doing it		Delegating	Budgeting		
Good at this, feel capable doing it		Mediating	Writing		
Needs work or training to improve		Mentoring	Mechanical		
Needs work or training to improve		Yoga	Managing Change		
Needs work or training to improve	Counselling/Coaching	Negotiating	Creating online content	Dealing with Public criticism	Selling
Needs work or training to improve			Researching	Making things	
Complete disaster at this				Implementing	

Unless you can really build a viable case for the items that find themselves on this list, e.g. *Will help me stay safe and save lives when the next earthquake hits,* I suggest giving no more of your time or energy to these items; it's time to ditch these activities!

Note: In a curious way, we tend to assume that we *like* the things we are good at so doing this exercise will help to shed some of our own illusions to get to the core of things we actually *enjoy* doing, even if we are completely inexperienced in doing them – it is a case of eking out those activities we are drawn towards because we want to learn more, hone them or even become an expert in them that will help us find our true path – in short, run with open arms towards the things that motivate you and steer away from those that either bore you to tears or get you down, even if you are really good at doing them!

APPENDIX C

Using the inter-relationship diagram to solve life issues

This is a very useful tool if you want to understand the relationship between issues or problems in your life and their underlying motivations or symptoms that need to be addressed. I use an example to show you how this tool can be effective in helping you problem solve and understand your underlying motivations.

Step 1: Define the problem – here we identify the issue you feel is most at play in your life right now by writing out your problem statement at the top of a blank page:

Example: *'I am terrified at starting my own business.'*

Step 2: Brainstorm possible causes – write down anything that springs to mind on Post-it notes or individual pieces of paper (so you can move them around).

Example responses to the statement above could include:

'Don't have enough money'

'Don't know how to go about it'

'Need for security'

'Lack of family support

'Mortgage'

Step 3: Identify the cause and its effects – for each item found in Step 2, identify if it is the cause of the issue or the symptom. For example, 'mortgage' could be a cause of 'don't have enough money' and itself a symptom of 'need for security'. Draw arrows between your cause and effects: you may find more than one relationship here, as in the example below, so take time to review each in turn to bottom out.

Note – you can also consider using solid or dotted arrows to indicate the strength of your relationship if you want to attach more meaning in your diagram.

Step 4: Identify the key drivers and outcomes – by counting the number of arrows into and out of each issue/effect, we can sift out the key drivers and outcomes.

The issues with the highest number of arrows OUT are your key drivers. The effects with the highest number of arrows IN are you key outcomes. Here we are identifying the most significant causes of your problem statement.

So, per our example, we see that '*Need for security*' has two arrows *out* so this is your key driver or motivator, and '*Insecure about taking the next step*' has three arrows *in* so this is the key outcome or effect in your life.

You can even plot them on a graph to make this more visual:

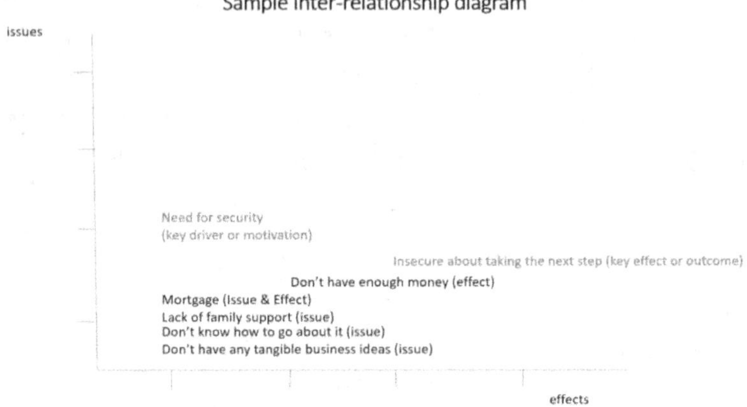

Step 5: Identify how to solve or work through the key problems – this is the most important step where you help yourself by coming up with ways to tackle the blocking issues and their effects.

Using our example, you may decide to address your issues and outcomes as follows:

- Save money to allow you to transition in a comfortable manner – maybe look at how to address your mortgage concern, e.g. downsizing, taking in a lodger, etc

- Secure external funding to help you start up your own business, e.g. working with a local enterprise program, crowd-funding, getting investors onboard, etc

- Take a start-up business training course to help you identify the steps you need to take to empower yourself and build your family's trust in what you are doing

EPILOGUE

A question from my friends has made me stop and think – was it all worth it? They mean all the upheaval, such as pulling the mat of stable income from under my family's feet, leaving myself vulnerable and out of kilter with the rest of my working community who predominantly work in senior corporate roles and who may see this book as an attack on their life choices and lifestyle. I have to say a resounding *yes* – for me, it *has* been worth it. The soul search in itself has shown me new ways of looking at the world that would never have been illuminated had I not stepped off the hamster-wheel. Like in the film *The Matrix*, you may actively choose to take the blue pill and stay blissfully unaware within the corporate scheme of things, or take the red pill which will project you down a rabbit hole, exposing some discomfiting truths about yourself and the choices you make along the way. It has to be said, though, that I have never felt more alive, more aware and more conscious than I do today and that for me makes the transition all worthwhile. I feel I have grown as a person, experienced new challenges and am conquering parts of my psyche that were holding me back just so I could remain 'comfortable'.

More and more I would argue as a society we strive for that quiet, relaxed, cosy space that is comfort, just to get some time out, because I think we are all to some extent experiencing a mix of burnout and boreout from corporate-driven dependency. Deep down, I feel we know we are meant to be more than just existing to be the robots of tomorrow. Dealing first with the burnout will allow us eventually to step beyond a way of living which is a reaction to physical and mental exhaustion. We could, of course, just let the AI do all the controlling, whilst we devolve into passive automatons. It's a sure thing that this is where we are headed unless we make ourselves step off the wheel and get conscious – and we need to do this soon.

So, we need to really challenge ourselves to be braver and think bigger as we look further down the road of human existence at what this comfort-driven society is doing to humanity as a whole. As we wallow in our comfortable ruts, we need to consider who is holding the reigns, steering the course of our human journey – and that of our children – and exactly where we are going.

First, though, let's deal with corporate fatigue by working to eliminate the source of it, while getting fit and well. Then, when rested and energised you will find yourself ready to take the steps to figure out what parts you want to play in helping to build our next human chapter together.

I wish you well with your journey. Know that there is a better plan for you – one that will steer you towards being the best version of yourself.

What more can you possibly aspire to?

ACKNOWLEDGEMENTS

Thank you to my parents for anchoring the seeds of love, freedom, empathy and social justice within us and for emboldening me to challenge the status quo when needed.

Thank you to my family and friends for supporting me on this journey, which wasn't always smooth sailing. From my heart, I thank you for your patience, love and non-judgement as I worked to free myself. This transformation has enabled me to find peace within myself, where my life has regained its colour, meaning and joyfulness – for this I am truly and forever grateful.

Thank you my publishing team at KINDLE BOOK PUBLISHING for the production of this book.

BIBLIOGRAPHY

The Artist's Way by Julia Cameron

https://www.simplypsychology.org/maslow.html

The Future of Work by Sergio Caredda

https://sergiocaredda.eu/people/future-of-work/part-1-a-brief-history-of-work/

The Guardian article on 'The Literal Meaning of Work' by Jeremy Seabrook

https://www.theguardian.com/commentisfree/2013/jan/14/language-labouring-reveals-tortured-roots1#:~:text=The%20English%20%22work%22%20has%20an,bear%20down%20upon%20or%20compel

After Work: A history of the Home and the Fight for Free Time by Helen Hester and Nick Srnicek, published by Verson

Corporate Cults: The Insidious Lure of the All-Consuming Organisation by Dave Arnott

Meaning of Corporation and Multinationals:

https://en.wikipedia.org/wiki/Corporation#:~:text=The%20concept%20of%20the%20corporation%20was,body%20politic%20to%20describe%20the%20state.&text=The%20concept%20of%20the,to%20describe%20the%20state.&text=of%20the%20corporation%20was,body%20politic%20to%20describe

https://www.vocabulary.com/dictionary/corporation. Accessed 14 Jul. 2023 https://en.wikipedia.org/wiki/Multinational_corporation

A Treatise on the Law of Corporations by Stewart Kyd (1793–1794)

https://www.theenumeration.com/largest-companies-in-the-world/

https://en.wikipedia.org/wiki/List_of_largest_companies_by_revenue#External_links

Gallup 'State of the Workplace 2023' report

https://www.gallup.com/workplace/349484/state-of-the-global-workplace-2022-report.aspx

International Labour organisation view on work:

https://www.ilo.org/global/publications/world-of-work-magazine/articles/WCMS_091639/lang--en/index.htm

https://www.indeed.com/career-advice/career-development/what-are-corporate-jobs

www.Investopedia.com

OECDs 2019 'Owners of the World's Listed Companies' report: oecd.org/corporate/Owners-of-the-Worlds-Listed-Companies.pdf

Bullshit Jobs by David Graeber

https://en.m.wikipedia.org/wiki/Bullshit_Jobs

Definition of burnout: psychologytoday.com

Gallup discussion by Dr. Ben Wigert gallup.com: July 2023 Article from businessinsider.com on returning to the office

www.bbc.com/worklife/article/20230206-the companies-backtracking-on-flexible-work

The Burnout Epidemic: The Rise of Chronic Stress and How we can Fix It by Jennifer Moss

edenproject.com

https://www.mckinsey.com/industries/technology-media-and-telecommunications/our-insights/the-social-economy

neuroscience.stanford.edu/news/why-multitasking-does-more-harm-good

ABOUT THE AUTHOR

Y Not is a veteran of corporate life, having over 30 years experience across a broad range of sectors. Taking the decision to quit the corporate sphere following a final role as a senior ranking, global head of a large multinational sent shockwaves through every aspect of her life and its meaning, which in turn prompted her full transformation.

Sharing the journey are her life partner, teen children, a cat and a dog!

Y Not, through new eyes, now has the opportunity to seek out fresh experience, embracing a resplendent new life chapter of adventure coupled with the gift of 'paying it forward' whenever the opportunity arises.